First World War
and Army of Occupation
War Diary
France, Belgium and Germany

52 DIVISION
Divisional Troops
56 Brigade Royal Field Artillery
1 April 1918 - 31 March 1919

WO95/2892/3

The Naval & Military Press Ltd
www.nmarchive.com
Published in association with The National Archives

Published by

The Naval & Military Press Ltd

Unit 10 Ridgewood Industrial Park,

Uckfield, East Sussex,

TN22 5QE England

Tel: +44 (0) 1825 749494

www.naval-military-press.com

www.nmarchive.com

This diary has been reprinted in facsimile from the original. Any imperfections are inevitably reproduced and the quality may fall short of modern type and cartographic standards.

© **Crown Copyright**
Images reproduced by permission of The National Archives, London, England, 2015.

Contents

Document type	Place/Title	Date From	Date To
Heading	WO95/2892/3 56 Brigade Royal Field Artillery		
Miscellaneous	52nd Division 56th Brigade R.F.A. Apr 1918-Mar 1919 From EGYPT 7 (Meerut) Division		
Miscellaneous	52nd Divisional Artillery Disembarked Marseilles From Egypt 12.4.18 56th Brigade R.F.A. April 1918		
Heading	War Diary Of 56th Brigade R.F.A. From 1st May 1918 To 31st May 1918 Volume IV (Part V)		
Heading	War Diary Of 56th Brigade R.F.A. From 1st April 1918 To 31st April 1918 Volume IV (Part IV)		
War Diary	Moascar Ismailia	01/04/1918	03/04/1918
War Diary	Alexandria	03/04/1918	04/04/1918
War Diary	At Sea	04/04/1918	11/04/1918
War Diary	Marseilles	12/04/1918	18/04/1918
War Diary	Sailly-Le Sec	19/04/1918	26/04/1918
War Diary	In The Field	27/04/1918	30/04/1918
War Diary	Coupelle Neuf	02/05/1918	07/05/1918
War Diary	Liebessart	08/05/1918	31/05/1918
Miscellaneous	A.G 3rd Echelon	04/07/1918	04/07/1918
Heading	War Diary Of 56th Brigade R.F.A. From 1st June 1918 To 30th June 1918 Volume IV		
War Diary	Vimy	01/06/1918	30/06/1918
Heading	War Diary 56th Bde R.F.A. July 1st 1918 To July 31/1918 Vol IV Part VII		
War Diary	Vimy	01/07/1918	31/07/1918
Heading	War Diary Of 58th Brigade R.F.A. From-1st August 1918 Vol-IV Part VIII		
War Diary	Roclincourt	01/08/1918	16/08/1918
War Diary	Acq	17/08/1918	21/08/1918
War Diary	Mercatel	22/08/1918	28/08/1918
War Diary	Fontaine	29/08/1918	31/08/1918
Heading	War Diary Of 56th Bde R.F.A. September 1918		
Heading	War Diary Of 56th Brigade Royal Artillery From 1st September 1918 To 30th September 1918 Volume IV Part IX		
War Diary	Fontaine	01/09/1918	03/09/1918
War Diary	Pronville	03/09/1918	30/09/1918
Heading	War Diary Of 56th Brigade Royal Field Artillery September 1918		
Miscellaneous	A Form Messages And Signals		
Miscellaneous	C Form. Messages And Signals.	07/09/1918	07/09/1918
Miscellaneous	285th Brigade R.F.A.	03/09/1918	03/09/1918
Operation(al) Order(s)	57th Divisional Artillery Operation Order No. 31	01/09/1918	01/09/1918
Miscellaneous	In Connection With XVII Corps Order No. 155		
Map	Map		
Map	Sketch B		
Map	Map A		
Miscellaneous	52nd D.A.No.A/560	05/09/1919	05/09/1919
Miscellaneous	Night Concentrations		
Miscellaneous	63rd (R.N.) Divisional Artillery Instructions No.1	07/09/1918	07/09/1918
Miscellaneous	52nd D.A.No.A/565.	06/09/1918	06/09/1918

Miscellaneous	52nd D.A.No.A/560/1	05/09/1918	05/09/1918
Diagram etc	Diagram		
Miscellaneous			
Diagram etc	Diagram		
Miscellaneous	A Form Messages And Signals		
Miscellaneous	52nd D.A. No.A/567	07/09/1918	07/09/1918
Miscellaneous	C Form Messages And Signals	07/09/1918	07/09/1918
Miscellaneous	56th. Brigade No.R.14	06/09/1918	06/09/1918
Miscellaneous	56th. Bde No.R.14	08/09/1918	08/09/1918
Diagram etc	Diagram		
Miscellaneous	C Form Messages And Signals	09/09/1918	09/09/1918
Operation(al) Order(s)	57th Divisional Artillery Order No. 63	16/09/1918	16/09/1918
Diagram etc	Diagram		
Operation(al) Order(s)	63rd (R.N.) Divisional Artillery Operation Order No. 226	07/09/1918	07/09/1918
Operation(al) Order(s)	57th Divisional Artillery Order No. 61	09/09/1918	09/09/1918
Miscellaneous	Reference 57th Divisional Artillery Order No. 61	11/09/1918	11/09/1918
Operation(al) Order(s)	57th Divisional Artillery Operation Order No. 35.	10/09/1918	10/09/1918
Miscellaneous	6th Brigade R.F.A.	11/09/1918	11/09/1918
Operation(al) Order(s)	57th Divisional Artillery Operation Order No. 36	11/09/1918	11/09/1918
Operation(al) Order(s)	57th Divisional Artillery Operation Order No. 37	11/09/1918	11/09/1918
Miscellaneous	Notes On Employment Of Smoke Shell		
Miscellaneous	52nd D.A. No.A/631.	19/09/1918	19/09/1918
Miscellaneous	56th Bde R.F.A. Oct 1918		
Heading	War Diary From 1st October 1918 To 31st October 1918 56th Brigade R.F.A.		
War Diary	Cantaing	01/10/1918	06/10/1918
War Diary	Novelles	07/10/1918	08/10/1918
War Diary	Awoingt	09/10/1918	10/10/1918
War Diary	Vaques Bridge	11/10/1918	11/10/1918
War Diary	St Aubert	12/10/1918	17/10/1918
War Diary	Proville	18/10/1918	18/10/1918
War Diary	Vaux. Vraucourt	19/10/1918	20/10/1918
War Diary	La Targette	21/10/1918	23/10/1918
War Diary	Auby	24/10/1918	25/10/1918
War Diary	Fratsmarais	26/10/1918	31/10/1918
Operation(al) Order(s)	63rd (R.N.) Divisional Arty. Operation Order No. 3	01/10/1918	01/10/1918
Operation(al) Order(s)	52nd Divisional Artillery Order No. 40	03/10/1918	03/10/1918
Miscellaneous	9th Brigade Group Tasks		
Miscellaneous			
Miscellaneous	52nd D.A. A /675.	05/10/1918	05/10/1918
Miscellaneous	52nd D.A. No. S.O. 2922	05/10/1918	05/10/1918
Miscellaneous	63rd (R.N.) Divisional Artillery Instructions No. 1	06/10/1918	06/10/1918
Miscellaneous	Table "A" Creeping Barrage		
Diagram etc	Diagram		
Miscellaneous	A Form Messages And Signals		
Miscellaneous	63rd (R.N.) Divisional Arty. Instructions No.1.	06/10/1918	06/10/1918
Diagram etc	Diagram		
Miscellaneous	63rd (R.N.) Divisional Arty. Instructions No.1	07/10/1918	07/10/1918
Miscellaneous	63rd (R.N.) Divisional Arty. Instructions No.2	06/10/1918	06/10/1918
Miscellaneous		07/10/1918	07/10/1918
Miscellaneous	63rd (R.N.) Divisional Arty. Instructions No.2	07/10/1918	07/10/1918
Miscellaneous	52nd D.A. No.A/677	06/10/1918	06/10/1918
Miscellaneous	52nd D.A. No.Z/676	06/10/1918	06/10/1918
Miscellaneous	A Form Messages And Signals		
Miscellaneous	Locations Of 52nd Divisional Artillery	07/10/1918	07/10/1918

Miscellaneous	A Form Messages And Signals		
Miscellaneous	To All Recipients Of 63rd (R.N)Div.Arty. Instructions No.1.	07/10/1918	07/10/1918
Miscellaneous	Amendment No.3		
Miscellaneous		19/10/1918	19/10/1918
Miscellaneous	Acknowledge	18/10/1918	18/10/1918
Operation(al) Order(s)	52nd Divisional Artillery Order No. 44		
Operation(al) Order(s)	17th Infantry Brigade Order No. 253	12/10/1918	12/10/1918
Miscellaneous	56th. Brigade RFA MI/178	18/10/1918	18/10/1918
Operation(al) Order(s)	52nd Divisional Artillery Order No. 41	07/10/1918	07/10/1918
Miscellaneous	Strategical Move Of 52nd Divisional Artillery	18/10/1918	18/10/1918
Map	Map		
Miscellaneous	Map III 56 Bde		
Map	Map 2		
Map	Map		
Miscellaneous	Map II		
Map	Map		
Miscellaneous	Map I		
Miscellaneous	On His Majesty's Service.		
Miscellaneous	56 Bde RFA Vol 8		
Heading	War Diary Of 56th Brigade R.F.A. From-1st November 1918 To 30th November 1918 (Volume IV Part XI)		
War Diary	Samiand	01/11/1918	01/11/1918
War Diary	Mort. Du Proy	02/11/1918	08/11/1918
War Diary	Ban Secours	09/11/1918	10/11/1918
War Diary	Herchies	10/11/1918	13/11/1918
War Diary	Erbaut	14/11/1918	30/11/1918
Miscellaneous	War Diary For Month Of November 56th Bde RFA		
Operation(al) Order(s)	52nd Divisional Artillery Order No. 47	31/10/1918	31/10/1918
Miscellaneous	March Table		
Operation(al) Order(s)	12th Divisional Artillery Order No. 130	31/10/1918	31/10/1918
Miscellaneous	Issued With 12th Divisional Artillery Order No. 130		
Miscellaneous	Reference 52nd D.A. Order No. 47	31/10/1918	31/10/1918
Miscellaneous	12 D.A. No. R.A. 1075/1	02/11/1918	02/11/1918
Miscellaneous	C Form Messages And Signals	02/11/1918	02/11/1918
Miscellaneous	12 D.A. No. R.A. 1075	02/11/1918	02/11/1918
Miscellaneous	To O.C. A/63rd Brigade	02/11/1918	02/11/1918
Operation(al) Order(s)	52nd Divisional Artillery Order No. 50	04/11/1918	04/11/1918
Operation(al) Order(s)	156th Infantry Brigade Order No. 69	08/11/1918	08/11/1918
Operation(al) Order(s)	156th Infantry Brigade Order No. 51	05/11/1918	05/11/1918
Miscellaneous	BM 275	07/11/1918	07/11/1918
Miscellaneous	BI 259	05/11/1918	05/11/1918
Miscellaneous	412th Field Coy.R.E. BM 260	05/11/1918	05/11/1918
Miscellaneous	O.C. 4th Royal Scots BM 263	05/11/1918	05/11/1918
Miscellaneous	4th Royal Scots	05/11/1918	05/11/1918
Miscellaneous	C Form Messages And Signals		
Miscellaneous	C Form Messages And Signals	07/11/1918	07/11/1918
Miscellaneous	C Form Messages And Signals	08/11/1918	08/11/1918
Miscellaneous	B.M.1/13	10/11/1919	10/11/1919
Map	Map		
Map	Belgium And Part Of France		
Miscellaneous	Map IV		
Map			
Map	Belgium And Part Of France		
Miscellaneous	Map V		

Heading	War Diary Of 56th Brigade R.F.A. From 1st December 1918 To 31st December 1918		
War Diary	Erbaut	01/12/1918	12/12/1918
War Diary	Casteau	12/12/1918	31/12/1918
Heading	War Diary Of 56th Brigade RFA From 1st January 1919 To 31st January 1919 (Volume V) Part I		
War Diary	Casteau	01/01/1919	29/01/1919
Heading	War Diary Of 56th Brigade R.F.A. From 1st February 1919 To 28th February 1919 Volume 5 Part II		
War Diary	Casteau	01/02/1919	28/02/1919
Heading	War Diary Of 56th Brigade RFA From 1st March 1919 To 31st March 1919 Volume V		
Miscellaneous	Extract From 52nd D.A No. S.C.309.		
War Diary	Casteau	01/03/1919	31/03/1919

WO95/2892/3
56 Brigade Royal Field Artillery

52ND DIVISION

56TH BRIGADE R.F.A.
APR 1918-MAR 1919

FROM ~~MESOPOTAMIA~~
~~VIA EGYPT~~

FROM EGYPT 7 (MEERUT) DIVISION

52nd Divisional Artillery.

Disembarked MARSEILLES from EGYPT 12.4.18.

56th BRIGADE R. F. A.

APRIL 1918.

Vol. 2

Confidential
WAR DIARY
of
5th Brigade R.F.A.

From 1st May 1918   To 31st May 1918

Volume IV (Part V)

In 9 grams

Adjt J.S.R.M.
Comg 5th Bde R.F.A.

Confidential
War Diary
of
56th Brigade R.F.A.

From 1st April 1918   to 30th April 1918.

(Volume Nº IV)

Ingram
Lt Col. Colonel R.A.
Comdg 56th F.A. Brigade

14 Vol 1 - 52

Confidential
War Diary

56th Brigade R.F.A.

From 1st April 1918   To 30th April 1918

(Volume IV pt. IV)

Th Ingram
The a/ Colonel R.A.
Comdg 56th Inf. Brigade R.

Confidential

Army Form C. 2118.

Instructions regarding War Diaries and Intelligence
Summaries are contained in F. S. Regs., Part II,
and the Staff Manual, respectively. Title pages
will be prepared in manuscript.

WAR DIARY
OR
INTELLIGENCE SUMMARY.

(Erase heading not required.)

Vol IV Part IV

56th Brigade
RFA

Hour. Date. Place.	Summary of Events and Information.	Remarks and references to Appendices.
MOASCAR ISMAILIA April 1st	527 Battery RFA rejoined Brigade 10pm 31-3-18 handed all horses & harness into remounts & ordnance. "C" Battery R.F.A. rejoined Brigade complete with same 6 Officers & 12 B.O.R's of 53rd Bde H.Q. posted to 527. Battery R.F.A.	JnJ
April 2nd	B.O.R's 72 + Followers 49 sent to KANTARA & struck off strength.	JnJ
April 3rd JnJ	All Batteries & Brigade HQ entrained MOASCAR for ALEXANDRIA. Brigade came on Port VII Establishment	
ALEXANDRIA April 3rd	Arrived ALEXANDRIA & whole Brigade with all technical vehicles embarked on S.S. MANNETOU. Captain L.S. Lloyd T.RFA, Lt H E Weld "Lt E Parrott with 62 B.O.R's rejoined Brigade & posted to 527. Battery R.F.A. 527 Battery RFA drew guns & wagons making up to 6 9 un Establishment 2Lt Tigar R.F.A. posted to "C" Battery RFA on 2nd	JnJ
April 4th	Sailed 1700 hours 2Lt Donnan R.FA transferred to "A" Battery RFA from 527 Battery RFA	JnJ
AT SEA April 5th 6th	NIL	JnJ

Confidential

Vol IV Part IV

Army Form C. 2118.
56th (Brigade)
RFA

WAR DIARY
or
INTELLIGENCE SUMMARY.
(Erase heading not required.)

Instructions regarding War Diaries and Intelligence Summaries are contained in F. S. Regs., Part II, and the Staff Manual, respectively. Title pages will be prepared in manuscript.

Hour. Date, Place.		Summary of Events and Information.	Remarks and references to Appendices.
AT SEA	April 7th to 11th	Nil	
MARSEILLES	April 12th	Arrived Marseilles. Started unloading	
	April 13th	Entrained MARSEILLES 23 B.O's, 849 B.O.R's (includes C.R.A's men) & all guns of Battery with all wagons of firing Battery ready. 6 officers in first class coach. Men in trucks. Horse & Mules rations on board. 4 days rations. via JUVISY & AMIENS.	
	April 14th & 15th	Steamed on	
	April 16th	Arrived Noyelles (10 kilos from ABBÉVILLE) Detrained. No sick. M.A. A & 527 Battery. H.Q. went into billets at SAILLY-LE-SEC. B Battery to Gunnery School Camp C Battery to FL. Beaucourt. B Battery to NOLLETTES	
	April 17th	6 officers & 2 Tommy O.C. 42	
	April 18th	Short inspection of vehicles	

W.O.I 42

Confidential.

56th Brigade Army Form C. 2118.
R.F.A.

WAR DIARY
OR
INTELLIGENCE SUMMARY. Vol II Part II

(Erase heading not required.)

Instructions regarding War Diaries and Intelligence Summaries are contained in F. S. Regs., Part II, and the Staff Manual, respectively. Title pages will be prepared in manuscript.

Hour. Date. Place.	Summary of Events and Information.	Remarks and references to Appendices.
SAILLY - LE - SEC April 19.	Horses obtained for A & B Batteries 1647 each & HQ 22 animals	727
April 20th	Horses drawn for C & 527 Batteries	779
" 21st	166	
" 24th	NIL	
" 25th	HQ signallers transferred to R.E. 1 Cpl. 1 B.^r	779
	1 B.^r 8 gunners & 3 Drivers Captain	
	Purcell A.V.C. attached to Brigade.	779
" 26th	NIL	779
" 27th	Brigade marched to & went into billets at WAVANS	779
	3 miles from AUXI-LE-CHATEAU	
" 28th	Marched to & went into billets at OEUF 6 miles	779
	from ST POL	
" 29th	Marched to & went into billets at COURELLE NEUF	779
	from FRUGES	
In the Field 30th	NIL	779
	J. L. Ingram	
	Lt Col. Bde	
	Comdg 56 RFA.	

Army Form C. 2118.

56th Brigade RFA
Vol III
Part IV

WAR DIARY
OR
INTELLIGENCE SUMMARY.
(Erase heading not required.)

Hour, Date, Place.	Summary of Events and Information.	Remarks and references to Appendices.
May 1st COUPELLE NEUVE	NIL	JR.9
2nd	Lt Wood B/56 posted as a/Captain to 9th Brigade RFA & struck off strength.	JR.9
3rd	5 Officers & 16 O.R's attached 256th Brigade RFA 51st Division. This party returned on the 6th	JR.9
4th	NIL	JR.9
5th	Lt E Madgwick R.E attached to Bde H.Q. in charge of signallers	JR.9
6th	4 Officers & 16 O.R's attached 51st Division	JR.9
7th	NIL	JR.9
8th	At 18 hr completed with oil tanks & went into billets at	JR.9
LIEBESSART	Brigade marched 4 miles N.W. of ST POL.	
	LIEBESSART about	
	Lt H. Bibby S.R RFA joined & posted to 'A' Battery	
	Lt R.D. Foxley S.R. RFA joined & posted to 'B' Battery	JR.9
	Lt C. Bullock Ty. RFA. joined & posted to 'C' Battery	
9th	Last party returned from attachment to 51st Division	JR.9
10,11,12	NIL	

Army Form C. 2118.

56th Brigade. R.F.A.
56th Brigade R.F.A.
Vol IV
Part 5

WAR DIARY
OR
INTELLIGENCE SUMMARY.
(Erase heading not required.)

Hour, Date, Place.	Summary of Events and Information.	Remarks and references to Appendices.
13th May	H.Q. A B & 527 Batteries marched q. went into billets at TENEUR in order to be near water	JL 9
14th "	All Egyptian Ammunition changed for French	JL/
15th "	Marched & went into Billets at CHELERS	JL/
16th "	Marched & went into huts at VILLERS-au-BOIS 6 Miles N.W. of ATTAS XVIII Corps area	JL/
17th "	Rec'd 2 Officers ren. Battery & proportion of signallers & N.F.O's visited front returning on 21st. Major Clayton Northumberland Hussars joined as horseman	JL/
18th "	Lt Col Ingram Bfawrth O.C. q th Brigade R.F.A. reconnoitred for gun positions immediately S. of THELUS.	JL 9
19th "	All Batteries calibrated near GOUAY-SERVINS	JL 9
20th "	NIL	
22nd "		
23rd "	Batteries sent one section each to relieve 65 th Army Brigade behind Vimy Ridge	JL 9
24th "	Relief completed as under Ref maps 36 C & B, 51 B & C	JL 9
	1/40000	

Army Form C. 2118.

56th Brigade R.F.A.
Vol IV Part V

WAR DIARY

INTELLIGENCE SUMMARY.
(Erase heading not required.)

Hour, Date, Place.	Summary of Events and Information.	Remarks and references to Appendices.
May 24th	A/56 A 6 Z 27.63 (5 guns) O.P. B 1 Z 2.3	Wagon line W 30 Z
	T 28 c 25.86 (1 gun)	Jh.?
	C/56 S 28 Z 62.11 (5 guns) O.P. A 6 Z 80.80	- ditto -
	T 20 d 80.35 1 gun	
	The above grouped with 52nd F.A. Brigade under Lt Col Thornycroft 52nd Brigade R.F.A.	
	B/56 S 22 d 35.19 (5 guns) O.P. S 23 c 30.20	Wagon line W 30/Z
	T 19 A 50.80 (1 gun)	
	527 S 28 Z 71.93 (6 How) O.P. S 22 Z 87.65	Wagon line W 30/Z
	T 19 a 35.80 (1 How)	
	H.Q. S 27 Z 00.60	Wagon line W 30 Z
	The above grouped with 242 F.A. Brigade under Lt Col Cockraft R.F.A. Both Groups supporting 52nd Division.	
	No. RFA / 110285 G. T. Millard & 2620 G. S. Hop Kins both of B/56 Bde R.F.A. Killed in action	
25th	NiL	
26th	NiL	
27th	2Lt T. Dunn S.R. RFA joined 22nd & posted to 'B' Battery	JU / JU / JU

Army Form C. 2118.

56th Bde. RFA

WAR DIARY
INTELLIGENCE SUMMARY.
(Erase heading not required.)

Vol II Part V

Hour, Date, Place.	Summary of Events and Information.	Remarks and references to Appendices.
May 28th & 31st	Nil	Nil
May 29th	Captain Miller A/56th Bde. RFA struck off strength S/25770	Nil
	A, B & C Batteries moved wagon lines to F11d 30/90, S.26 a.1.1 & A.2 a.1.9.0. respectively. HQ. to S 26 c 2.9.	Nil
May 30th & May 31st	Nil	
	Batteries 5 inch Laid 5 guns Map	
	A/56 A6 d 25 7.63 1 Gun Tank Gun	
	B/56 S 22 d 35.19 T26 c 25.88 B.16 1.7	
	C/56 A5 d 61.34 T19 a 50.80 T19 d 77.75	
	527 S 28 b 28.84 T25 d 05 85 nil	
	T19 a 35 80 T19 c 75.95	
	Ammunition fired during month as below. as per attached Telew	Nil
	A Ax	
	A/56 451 490	
	B/56 646 307	
	C/56 102 251	
	1199 Bx 1048	
	527 Battery 624 Brc 96	
	Total Rds 2967	

Th. Ingram
Lt Col
Condg 56th Bde
RFA

2-6-18

6

A.G.
3rd Echelon

Herewith War Diary
for June for 56th Bde
R.G.A.

Butters
Major for a/Col
Comdg. 56 Bde R.G.A.

4/7/18

Vol 3

52.

Confidential

War Diary

56th Brigade R.F.A.

From 1st June 1918   To 30th June 1918

Volume IV part VI

Minnieuwe

Major R.F.A.
Comdg 56th Bde R.F.A.

56th Bde RFA
Vol VI Part VII

WAR DIARY
INTELLIGENCE SUMMARY
(Erase heading not required.)

Hour, Date, Place.	Summary of Events and Information.	Remarks and references to Appendices.
VIMY June 1st	177 Howr exchanged for 177 Howrs with 9th Brigade RFA	
June 2nd	No 2728 Dr. J.E. Black from 527 Battery RFA wounded	JV.1
June 5th	No 124788 UB. Mayes A/56 wounded "Gas"	JV.1
	No 229475 Gr. B. Johnson C B/56 wounded	JV.1
June 6th	Lt E R Bartlett 527 Battery RFA struck off strength	JV.1
	of Brigade & Capt G.J. Miller RFA struck off strength of Brigade from May 29th prox.	
	Lt E C H Jensen promoted acting Captain whilst 2nd in command of A/56th Bde RFA	
June 7th & 8th	No 22453 Cpl Fletcher W c/56th Bde RFA wounded	JV1
June 8th to 13th	N.L. Genl Fasson B.G.R.A 18th Corps inspected A & B Batteries	
	2/Lt J.D. Dornan transferred from A Battery to	JV.1
14th	52nd D.A.C. & struck off strength accordingly	
	D.A.C. Gnrs C. & No 1115758 Gr. Reay H wounded both	
15	No 891454 Cpl Gnus C. & No 1115758 Gr. Reay H wounded both	
	2/Lt J.M. Bury RFA SR joined & posted to A Battery	JV1
	2/Lt W. Beynon RFA SR joined & posted to B Battery	
	Gen Fasson B.G.R.A 18th Corps inspected C & 527 Batteries	

Army Form C. 2118.

56th Brigade RFA
Vol IV Part II

WAR DIARY
or
INTELLIGENCE SUMMARY.
(Erase heading not required.)

Hour, Date, Place.	Summary of Events and Information.	Remarks and references to Appendices.
Vimy June 16th	NIL	JL9
June 17th	NIL	JL9
June 18th	No 75583 G+W Fletcher A/56 wounded	JL1
June 19th	NIL	ditto
June 20th	NIL	ditto
June 21st–27th	NIL	ditto
June 28th	Capt A C G Lanclin way C/56 to hospital ill	ditto
June 29th	A and C/56 completed move from R+ Sweep	ditto
June 30th	6 Siege of Group. 35 ORs joined during the month. Batteries retaliated as below. 1 gun	Very
	A/56 S29c37.85 NIL	
	B/56 S22c86.14 T13c20.75	
	C/56 S28t60.24 T13c2475	
	527 S28t50.96 T19a35.80	
	Ammunition fired during the month	
	A/56 A 1363 AX 1206	
	B/56 " 2622 " 1929	
	C/56 " 1530 " 871	
	527 Bx 3111 BxC 510	

30-6-18 WJSturgeon Major comd 56 Bde RFA

War Diary
56th Bde R.J.A.

July 1st 1918
to
July 31/1918

Vol IV   Part VII

56 Bde 4

Army Form C. 2118.

56th Brigade R.F.A.
Vol IV Part VII

WAR DIARY
INTELLIGENCE SUMMARY.
(Erase heading not required.)

Instructions regarding War Diaries and Intelligence Summaries are contained in F. S. Regs., Part II. and the Staff Manual respectively. Title pages will be prepared in manuscript.

Place	Date	Hour	Summary of Events and Information	Remarks and references to Appendices
VIMY	July 1st	NIL		m.t
"	July 2nd	NIL		m.t
"	July 3rd Ld 6	NIL		JT.1
"	4th #1		H.Q. 56th Brigade R.F.A. took over left Group 52nd D.A. Comp.ed as follows:	
"	5th		56th Brigade R.F.A. B.242, D.242, B.242, supporting 157 Infantry Brigade. H.Q. at S.27.00.60.	JT.2
"	6th	NIL		JT.2
"	8th			JT.1
"	9th	NIL		JT.1
"	10th			JT.1
"	15th		Division First reconstructed left Section having only 1 Battalion in front line. Artillery supporting left Brigade consequently reduced to 56th Brigade R.F.A.	JT.1
"	16th			JT.1
"	17th	NIL		JT.1
"	18th		Maj. General Alexander R.A. 1st Army visited Batteries	JT.2
"	19th		No 123220 Gr. Jeffries W.E. A/56 slightly wounded by shell on 18th 5 Officers reconnoitred G.H.Q. line in vicinity of CAMLIN ABBEY & AUBIGNY	JT.1
"	20th		Orders for relief of 52nd D.A. received 56th Brigade R.F.A. relieved by 45th Brigade R.F.A. 8th Division	
"	21st		Relief completed Batteries rested for night in teams wagon lines	

Army Form C. 2118.

56th Brigade RFA
Vol IV Part VII

WAR DIARY
or
INTELLIGENCE SUMMARY.
(Erase heading not required.)

Instructions regarding War Diaries and Intelligence Summaries are contained in F. S. Regs., Part II. and the Staff Manual respectively. Title pages will be prepared in manuscript.

Place	Date	Hour	Summary of Events and Information	Remarks and references to Appendices
VITRY July 21st 1918			a Capt. J. G. Fuller RFA rejoined and posted to A/56 Battery RFA. 2 Lt S. C. Brown RFA joined & posted to 527 Battery RFA. a Capt E C H Jensen RFA transferred from A/56 to B/56 Battery RFA.	Th.1 Th.2
July 22nd			Brigade marched to and went into camp at Bois de HAZOIS. 2 Miles West of HOUDAIN & came under orders of XVII" Corps	Th.2
July 23rd to 24th			N.L	Th.2 Th.2
July 25th			Brig. Gen Willis B.G. R.A. Corps visited Batteries Maj. Gen Vaughan Chief Horsemaster G.H.Q inspected the horses of the Brigade	Th.2
July 26th			Brigade moved to Billets in Clá/18 Division	Th.2
July 27th			Owing to continued rain	Th.2
July 28th			Brigade rested	
July 29th			Orders received to relieve 5" C.D.A just North of Arras. Wagon Lines Brigade marched 7am & relieved forward sections between MAROEUIL & ROCLINCOURT.	Th.1 Th.1
July 30th			Relief completed commands passing on right at 30/31 Th.1 as follows.	

Army Form C. 2118.

Confidential

WAR DIARY
or
INTELLIGENCE SUMMARY.
(Erase heading not required)

Vol. IV Part VII 56th Bde R.F.A.

Place	Date	Hour	Summary of Events and Information	Remarks and references to Appendices
July 30th			On completion of relief Brigade situated as follows	
				Relieved Forward guns Wagon line
			56th Bde R.F.A. HQ	14th Bde C.F.A. G.56.30.15 L.6c.59.90
			A/56 R.F.A.	60th Bty C.F.A. A.30.c.30.00 B.26.d.24.80 L.10.b.92.80
				5 guns 1 gun
			B/56 R.F.A.	61st Bty C.F.A. A.30.c.24.29 B.25.d.65.65 F.23.d.80.50 Tu.
				4.5 guns 2 guns
			C/56 R.F.A.	66th Bty C.F.A. A.30.c.41.84 B.26.b.00.00 F.29.c.92.60
				4 guns B.28.b.70.30
				2 guns
			527 R.F.A.	58th Bty C.F.A. A.29.d.49.70 B.1.b.39.15 G.8.a.40.30
				4.9 guns 2 guns
			Sheet 51B N.W. Edition 10	
July 31st			52nd Can. Division Infantry with 57th Division relieve 4th Canadian Division	J.I.9.
			Ammunition fired during July	
			18 pr 4.5 How BAA CRB A.S.
			A A.X BX 78 2 9
			7068 3469 3190
			Total 13816 Rounds
			Reinforcements received during the month 25 6 other Ranks
			A quiet month. J.N. Ingrain Lt. Col. 31-7-18
			Comdg 56th Bde R.F.A.

CONFIDENTIAL.
****

ORIGINAL.

Vol 5

WAR DIARY OF

56TH BRIGADE R.F.A.

VOL.- IV.
PART - VIII.

FROM - 1st AUGUST 1918.   TO - 31st AUGUST 1918.

Confidential

Army Form C. 2118.

56th Brigade RFA
Vol IV Part 8

WAR DIARY
INTELLIGENCE SUMMARY.
(Erase heading not required.)

Place	Date	Hour	Summary of Events and Information	Remarks and references to Appendices
ROCLINCOURT	1-8-18		No 59889 L/Bdr Baughan W } wounded	J.9
			" 126326 Gnr Gray AM } B/56 Battery	
			" 179107 G. Rogers H.F } Hospital "shock"	
			" 188367 G. Beddall D }	
			" 119710 G. Hughes E }	
	2-8-18		No 104701 Cpl Lewis T B/56 Battery wounded	J.9
	3-8-18 to 7-8-18		Nil 527 Battery with 28th Battery RFA	J.9
	8-8-18		Brigade supports 156th Infantry Brigade from present positions	
	9-8-18 to 10-8-18		NIL	
	11-8-18		No 3168 Sergt Pose G.W. and no 1137555 Gnr Shinn R.J. Killed	—
			" 90961 J/BM Howell A.H. and 141968 Gnr Hawkins W.H. attended	
			Three of the men were of C/56 and the casualties occurred when	
			the B.H.Q. forward section was heavily shelled G.5.9.i.	
	12-8-18 to 14-8-18		NIL	—
	15-8-18		Bde withdrew from the forward section in return near ROCLIN COURT to wagon lines.	
	16-8-18		Bde marched from to gun line to ACq.	—

Confidential

6/6th R.B.

Army Form C. 2118.

Instructions regarding War Diaries and Intelligence Summaries are contained in F.S. Regs., Part II. and the Staff Manual respectively. Title pages will be prepared in manuscript.

WAR DIARY
INTELLIGENCE SUMMARY.
Vol IV part 8

(Erase heading not required)

Place	Date	Hour	Summary of Events and Information	Remarks and references to Appendices
ACQ	17-8-18 to 20-8-18		In billets in ACQ	
	21-8-18		Bn marches to BEAUMETZ	
MERCATEL	22-8-18		Bn went into action in M34c	
	23-8-18		Bn in front of attack by 52 Divn trops at 4.55 am	
	24-8-18		Bn engaged in front of attack by 52 Divn trops in M34a (15 Crandallie) street	
			A Armoured and occupied position in M34a. Hughes wounded.	
"	25-8-18	5 am	B withdrew Bn to front now in M34c	
"	26-8-18		B Bn advanced to M36a (a+B+c) and M35b (G)K+1527/35).	
		ar 10 pm	to support attack on Hindenburg Line.	
"	27-8-18	At 8 pm	B Bn advanced to T2a and T9a found barrage at 10 am	
	28-8-18	at 10.30 am	R Bn advanced to H35d and R Bn advanced to A56+R/56 advanced to U10 and were in the afternoon Shelled Selling into action	

WAR DIARY

Army Form C. 2118.

6(Ba) R7a
Vol IV Part 8

INTELLIGENCE SUMMARY.

(Erase heading not required)

Place	Date	Hour	Summary of Events and Information	Remarks and references to Appendices
Fontaine	29-8-18	at 6am	527 R.F. returned to V7b 7.4. and 6/56b.	
		07a 4.2 at 9am	Captain Neill 1/C/56 severely wounded	
			Lt Browne 6/7 R.F. heavily behaved killed whilst	
			Fwd dig	
	30-8-18		Same conditions — quiet day	
	31-8-18		ditto.	

The following casualties occurred during the month —

KILLED. 3168. Bdr Fay, En. B/56. 40185. Dvr Allard. 9 B/56. 1760. Sgt Donnell, R. 52+B/y.
107249, Dvr ——— 113mH, Sgt. 52+B/y. 113455 Gnnr Stevens, R.g. B/56.
WOUNDED. 59289 2/A/Bmbr Naughton, W. B/56. 126326 Gnr Gurg, a.m. B/56. 149107 Gnr Rogers. H.Q. B/56.
18364 Gnr Bastanes, R. B/56. 104704 A/B Lewis. J. 52+B/y. 114430 Gnr Roberts. A/56.
91461 L/Bmr Ruseley, A.H. B/56. 149168 Gnr Matthias. CH B/56. 52+53 Sgt Emery Jo. B/56. 92076 Gnr Ince. 2B/56.
117460 Gnr Roberts. O. A/56. 167184 Gnr Lendersomb. H.Q/56. 131791 Gnr Gunner. 6 B/56.
104493 Gnr Vaughan. 3 B/56. 86572 L/Cpl Hellier B/56. 137807 Gnr Chapman. 6 B/56. 137758.
97192 Gnr Shannon, 3 B/56. 47758 Gnr Thomas W. B/56. 145514 Gnr Hynner B./C/56.
8664 Bpl. Elmer W. B/56. 90776 Gnr Gurling D. C/56. 10987 Gnr Shilton B./C/56.
101699 Dry Smithson R. C/56. 7"573 Dr Emoth Mrs. J. B/56. 9:57bd Sgt Hyde (actng) A/56.
107928 Gnr Ilin. CO. A/56. 45760 Am Griffin. J. A/56. ^ 69473 Gnr Love R. A/56.
50760 Gdr Cousin. J. B/56. 103660 Gnr Dawson H. B/56. 41438 L/Sgt Warren R.y. B/56.

Army Form C. 2118.

56th Bde R.F.A.

Vol IV Part 8

WAR DIARY
or
INTELLIGENCE SUMMARY.
(Erase heading not required.)

Instructions regarding War Diaries and Intelligence Summaries are contained in F. S. Regs., Part II. and the Staff Manual respectively. Title pages will be prepared in manuscript.

Place	Date	Hour	Summary of Events and Information	Remarks and references to Appendices

Commencement of Conversion — August 1918.

2619 Gnr Evans J. 8/56. 47302 Gnr Tarlun G. 8/56. 116390 Dr Harris, H. A/56 8/56
35209 Bdr Smith 8/56. 8/56. 141102 Dr Coddrington Jno 8/56. 11209 Dr Rose W. B/56
96657 Dr Goode H. D/56. 261418 Dr Watts. W. C/56. 140967 Dr Duncan 521B/y
99901 Sgt Wrigglesworth H. 521B/y. 33070 Gnr Will J. 521B/y. 9729 Gnr Farmiloe G. 521B/y
46159 Gnr Brian J. 10/56. 141166 Gunner Simmons J. 8/56. 45969 Gunner ——

Montrevin
M.F.P.

Cmdy 66 Bde R.F.A.

On His Majesty's Service.

52nd Dv

War Diary
of
56th Bde: R.F.A.

September 1918

CONFIDENTIAL.
===

ORIGINAL.
===

Vol 6

WAR DIARY OF 56th BRIGADE ROYAL ARTILLERY.
===

VOLUME IV.
PART - IX.
===

FROM -
1ST SEPTEMBER 1918.

TO -
30th SEPTEMBER 1918.

WAR DIARY

56th Brigade R.F.A.
Vol IV Part 9

Army Form C. 2118.

Instructions regarding War Diaries and Intelligence Summaries are contained in F.S. Regs., Part II. and the Staff Manual respectively. Title pages will be prepared in manuscript.

Place	Date	Hour	Summary of Events and Information	Remarks and references to Appendices
FONTAINE	1-9-18		Barrage at 4.50 am Infantry took Maeuvres Chateau. A B & C Btys moved to U 8 d	
	2-9-18		Barrage the DROCOURT-QUEANT Line at 5am. The 47 Div Infantry got through when V13 + V14 entered & bombed Cavite & B19 central about. The 63 Div Div Inf followed through punching Cavir See Appendix I	Appendix I Appendix II
	3-9-18		B de moved to V17 a at 4 pm. 63rd Division R.N. took over command of R.A. See Appendix II. B de moved to W27 a at noon	less
PRONVILLE			B de moved to [illeg] V17 a at 6 pm.	
	4-9-18		Lt Col J.H. Ingram R.F.A. rejoined from U.K. Germans counterattacked INCHY-EN-ARTOIS. Brigade replied to S.O.S. call 6pm. All quiet 7 pm. No RFA 108959 Q Cann R. C/56 Brigade R.F.A. wounded. No RFA 107549 D Bratt 9.9. 527 Battery R.F.A. Killed No RFA 107549 Cpl Jordan H.Q. 56th Bde. R.F.A. wounded Brigade locations as follows HQ 56th Bde RFA Ref 57c, NE A/56 Battery RFA B/56 " " C/56 " " 527 " "	Wagon line D 8 c + D 7 d Gun line 27 a + 6.16 B 60.40 D 17 a. 65.70 D 17 a. 50.60 D 17 a. 78.90 D 16 b 95.65

Confidential

WAR DIARY
or
INTELLIGENCE SUMMARY

56th Bde R.F.A.
Vol IV Part 9

Army Form C. 2118.

Place	Date	Hour	Summary of Events and Information	Remarks and references to Appendices
PRONVILLE	5.9.18		No R.F.A. 645336 Gr Gamble B/56 Battery R.F.A. wounded	II.9
			No R.F.A. 58138 Dr Waldron A/56 " " wounded	Appendix III & V
			Brigade in support of DRAKE Battalion 63rd Division & 7th Fusiliers 63rd Division see Appendices III & V	Appendix V
"	6.9.18		Brigade in support of Artists Rifles 63rd Division. None reported wounded	
			Lt Brown R.F.A. reported sick. Believed gassed.	Appendix XII
			Lt Doultwait R.F.A. to hospital	IV
			No R.F.A. 25994 Gr Wilson J wounded at duty A/56 Battery R.F.A.	
			70 miles received	
			34 Reinforcements to D 1 a c c ½ Ref 57c NE 20.000	Appendix VIII
"	7.9.18		Wagon lines moved to D 1 a c c ½ Ref 57c NE 20.000	IV
		5.30 p.m.	Barrage fired Appendix II. Gun & echelons full to be maintained.	
			Orders received for 300 rounds to be in	
			S.O.S lines as in Appendix XII	
			Capt. Purcell A.V.C. wounded at duty	
			527 Battery R.F.A. casualties	
			149556 Gr Bennett G. Killed	
			149454 Dr Newham B Killed	
			77075 Bomb: Stanton R. 89099 Bt Cook F.L. 106766 Dr Baxter. 154957 Dr Dismon	Appendix VIII
			Wounded 11524 Dr Evans W 129475 Dr Hannan F.T. 211174 Dr King J 126027 Dr Lamb J. 651521 Dr Vain	IV
			R61431 Dr Vala 213877 Dr Weston wounded	
"	8.9.18		C/56 Battery R.F.A. send forward 1 sniping section to D 17 Z 73.13.	Appendix IX
			see Appendix VIII Ref 57c NE 20.000	II.9
			63rd Division relieved by 57th Division see Appendix IX wounded	
			H.Q. moved to D 16 a. 20.75. Same reference	
			213877 Dr Weston 5170 L/B: Bodgen J B/56 wounded	

56th Brigade RFA
Vol IV Part IX

Army Form C. 2118.

WAR DIARY

INTELLIGENCE SUMMARY

Place	Date	Hour	Summary of Events and Information	Remarks and references to Appendices
PRONVILLE	10-9		Major A.L.E. Fleet R.F.A. Killed in action. B/56. 31363 Sgt Parker J.E. 119710 G: Hughes M. Killed. 40291 Sgt Connelly A. 42476 G: Cox A. 98431 a/10/Cpl Clifton L. wounded. B/56 moved D16c79.60 same reference. Brigade in support of 170 Brigade. B/56 moved D16c79.60 sea Appendices 10+11 Barrage fired for advance on canal DU NORD sea Appendix 11	J.W.J.
	11-9			
	12-9		Smoke screen fired an in Appendix D: Thorogeton J. 20th B/56 wounded. No 77337 D: Brigge E. No 91198 D: Martin J. 20th C/56 wounded. No 36240 Sgt Cooper L + A/B/B: Martin J. 20th C/56 wounded. SOS call for German counterattack on MOEUVRES answered. Brigade answered SOS lines from 6pm to 7.30 approximately.	J.W.J
	13-9		Brigade fired on MOEUVRES in reply to German trench mortars at request of infantry	
	14-9 3-7pm		Fired S.O.S in support of infantry attacked in MOEUVRE at 7.10 p.m. Attack repulsed. Map 57c.N.E. No 12256. Bombardier Cox. W. Wounded A/56. No: 118018. Gunner Hulme F Wounded. A/56. No 2621. Corporal Williams. T. wounded C/56. No 213974 Gunner Jones. T.E. wounded C/56.	Df

WAR DIARY

INTELLIGENCE SUMMARY.

56 Bde RFA

VOLUME IV PART IX

Place	Date	Hour	Summary of Events and Information	Remarks and references to Appendices
PRONVILLE	15/9		Lieut. E. Ward wounded (gassed) A/56.	G
	17/9		Fired S.O.S. in support of infantry. attacked in MOEUVRES 7-10 p.m. attack repulsed infantry positions consolidated Map ref. 57cNE. No 126336. Sergeant Gray .A.M. wounded. B/56 " 89208 Gunner Latham A. wounded at duty. C/56.	G
	18/9		Fired S.O.S. in support of infantry who were attacked in E14d at 5.5 pm for 15 minutes Map 57cNE. 2 Lieutenant Sidney Smithson joined and posted to A/56.	G
	19/9 /20		Fired barrage at 7.0 p.m. in accordance with Appendix. 12 in support of 155 Infantry Bde who attacked MOEUVRE for Capture. Attack helped up by T.M's at E30d 5.5 which were engaged by 527 How TM, after which attack was successful and objective gained. No. 19907 Gunner Baker P. gassed No 840680 Gunner Ten gassed No 56526 " O'Donnell. gassed No 72194 Gunner Manoles gassed all A/56. No 72704 Gunner. Colquhoun A. Wounded B/56.	G
	20/9		Lieut JOHN DUNN. B/56 wounded and missing believed killed No 140974 Driver Walker wounded 527 Hvwity Battery. Lieut Delaforce A/56 Posted to Portuguese Army Mission to fill Vacancy.	G

WAR DIARY

56 Bde R.F.A.

Army Form C. 2118.

INTELLIGENCE SUMMARY.   Volume IV   Part IX

Place	Date	Hour	Summary of Events and Information	Remarks and references to Appendices
PRONVILLE	21/9/18		56 Brigade R.F.A. in support of 156 Infantry Brigade. Fired S.O.S. 3.3 pm in support of infantry who were attacked in Ecod. Map 57cNE attack repulsed and line maintained. Casualties. Lieut. Iyson wounded (gassed). C/56. #391 Gunner Service V. No 19883 Gunner Bulayant 1 No 138-90 Corpl Harana Mal. W. No 91117 Sgt Stidmorr I No 92491 Sgt Cluff A. No 3/28 2/Br Hughes C. No 97227 2/Br Thomas J. No 27038 Gunner Coz. L. No 117313 Gunner Armitage F. No 107570 Gunner Brown J. No 91052 Gunner Cason MA. No 101167 Gunner Hardy H. No 94865 Gr. Harper G. No 242633 Gr Sutherland R No 91009 Gr Whitby W. No 137819 Gr Thompson E. No 1272 42 Bn Waugh. all A/56 wounded (gassed).	JG
	22/9/18		S.O.S. fired 8.51 pm E20 central no hostile barrage. SOS fired 9-4 pm in reply to intense Hostile Bombardment. Maps on Left of MOEUVRE. Map 57cNE. B/56 occupied position D17c 50.80 C/56 occupied position D17c 73.15. Ref Map 57cNE. Casualties. No 17294 Gunner Hillard J. wounded.	JG
	23/9/18		56 Brigade R.F.A. in support of 155 Infantry Brigade. 6-19 pm fired S.O.S. in reply to enemy shelling Front Line Captain CHARLES HUGH BRITAIN. Jones and 2/Lieut. JOSEPH Barlow joined and Posted #56 and attached A/56 and Posted to A/56.	JG

Army Form C. 2118.

Vol IV Part IX
56 Brigade R.F.A

WAR DIARY
or
INTELLIGENCE SUMMARY.
(Erase heading not required)

Place	Date	Hour	Summary of Events and Information	Remarks and references to Appendices
RONVILLE	23/9/18	—	No. 90972 Bombardier Brown T.W. Wounded B/56. No. 94935 Gunner Sygrove F. Wounded C/56	JG
	24th		2nd Lieut BRICE T.M. Joined and posted to B/56.	JG
	25th		6.7am to 6.45am fired S.O.S. in support of infantry. E20 6 + d Map 57 c N.E. Cavallia. No 95495. Bdr PYLE G.E. No 63418 Gunner Mallure W.F. Both B/56 wounded.	JG
	26th		Quiet day. Cavallia. No. 155900 Fitter Trick F.S. Wounded (gas) No 98567 Gunner Garner J.W. Wounded Both A/56. Received Notification of Zero hour for Barrage in support of Scheme to advance on line reconnoitred. No 18906 Dr R. Musgrove Killed. No 76746 Gr P Maunsell Wounded No 16648 Dr C.A. SHERRIE again wounded all A/56.	JG
	27"		5.20am batteries barrage CANAL DU NORD in support of 63rd Naval Division 7.0 am batteries advanced to position in E 25 d reference sheet 57 c NE 1:20000 and barraged GRAIN COURT. 5-0 pm batteries advanced and came into action just East of	

WAR DIARY
or
INTELLIGENCE SUMMARY.

Army Form C. 2118.

Vol IV Part IX
56 Brigade R.F.A.

Place	Date	Hour	Summary of Events and Information	Remarks and references to Appendices
HINDENBERG SUPPORT LINE	27		Casualties. Captain Kennick A.T. 507 wounded. No 27887 Gnr Brown M. No 146034 Gnr Redpath T. both 507 Battery. No 90513 Gr Tamms E. No 97536 Gr Middleton both B/56 Battery. No 4926 Gnr Butterworth H. No 131413 Gunner James R. No 97100 both of Bromyard 29/8 No reported *	* missing
	28	5.30am	Batteries barraged CHAINTAING in support of 57 Division.
		10.0am	Batteries advanced to positions in Sh 4 in support of 57 Division. 1 Section A/56 advanced in close support of 170 Infantry Bde 57 Division. This Section was withdrawn to main position at Dusk. Same day.
			Casualties. No 26567 Dr HARLOP J. A/56 No 83197 Dr FARME F.L. (No 96124) & FAIRER C.) wounded. 6519 Corpl CHAPLIN J. A/56 Accidently wounded.
	29		Batteries fired on PARIS COPSE WOOD in Sh 4 re reference sheet.
	30		57 to INN

JH Argument 2/ Col
Cmdg 56 Bde RFA

APPENDICES TO

WAR DIARY OF 56th BRIGADE ROYAL FIELD ARTILLERY.

SEPTEMBER 1918.

"A" Form.
MESSAGES AND SIGNALS.

Army Form C. 2121.
(In pads of 100.)

TO: 94 Bde.   285 Bde
    56? Bde

Sender's Number: F35
Day of Month: 1
AAA

Received definite orders for tomorrow's operations aaa The information just received supersedes all previous orders except that lifts of 45 hours during creeping barrage will still be from trench to trench aaa zero hour will be 5 am Sept 2nd aaa watches will have been synchronised by time these orders received aaa Acknowledge by [   ] pty wire

Place: Lt Group

(Z) [signature]

"C" FORM.
MESSAGES AND SIGNALS.

Prefix	Code	Words	Received. From RA By Floute	Sent, or sent out. At ... m. To ... By	Office Stamp. RA 7/9/18

Charges to Collect:
Service Instructions: SE2A Priority

Handed in at .... Office .... m. Received 2.57 m.

TO: SE2A

Sender's Number. F96	Day of Month. 7	In reply to Number.	AAA
Warning	Order	aaa	
creeping	barrage	will	be
fired	this	afternoon	aaa
starting	line	CANAL	DU NORD
lifts	200 yds.	parallel	to
canal	aaa	ammn.	about
50	rounds	per	gun
aaa	Details	at	present
on	their	way	from
63	D.A	aaa	no
Infantry	action	aaa	Brigade
Zones	will	be	H.F
Zones	aaa	Full	details
will	be	forwarded	as soon as
possible			

FROM PLACE & TIME: Left Group

SECRET.   App II

285th Brigade R.F.A.
286th   do.
5th Army Bde. R.F.A.
9th Brigade R.F.A.
—56th Brigade R.F.A.
57th Div. Ammn. Col.

    The command of the Field Artillery Group supporting the Left Division will be taken over by the C.R.A., 63rd Division from 1 pm. to-day.

    Headquarters, 63rd Divisional Artillery at U.7.d.6.8.

    57th Divisional Headquarters, and rear Artillery H.Q. will remain at N.28.c.4.4.

                                        Major,
                               a/Brigade Major, R.A.,
3/9/18.   57th Division.

SECRET.
******

D.A. 7/481.

Copy No. 21.

57th Divisional Artillery Operation Order No. 31.

1/September/1918.

Reference 57th Division Order No. 119 of to-day.
Following are orders for Left Division Artillery in support of this attack.

1. Maps showing Corps and Divisional Boundaries, Artillery Group and Brigade Boundaries, Objective Lines, and Barrage Areas, have been issued to Group Commanders.

2. DISTRIBUTION OF ARTILLERY.

RIGHT GROUP - Lieut-Colonel E.B. COTTER, D.S.O.

        5th Army Brigade R.F.A.
        286th Brigade R.F.A.

LEFT GROUP - Lieut-Colonel H.J. COTTER, C.I.E., D.S.O.

        9th Brigade R.F.A.
        56th Brigade R.F.A.
        285th Brigade R.F.A.

3. 1st BARRAGE.

18-PDRS. (a) At Zero hour a Creeping 18-pdr. Barrage will open on the line U.12.d.8.0. to U.30.b.80.45.
It will remain on this line until Zero plus 10, and will then lift back at rate of 100 yards every 3 minutes until Zero plus 19, when rate will be 100 yards every 5 minutes until Zero plus 84.

The boundaries for this barrage are -

On the North - The Corps Boundary.
On the South - The Divisional Boundary.
On the East - The Sunken Road from V.21.a.50.66. to V.28.b.90.20.

When each Battery reaches the Sunken Road (Eastern Boundary) or the boundary of its lane, it will continue searching all trenches in its particular lane until Zero plus 84, except in the area 200 yards South of the Corps Northern Boundary.

At Zero plus 84 - All 18-pdr. batteries will cease fire and will switch their lines of fire on to a line 200 yards South of the Corps Northern Boundary, with the exception of 286th Brigade R.F.A. which will be held in readiness to advance.

AMMUNITION - 45% Shrapnel.
                 40% H.E.
                 15% Smoke.

Flank Batteries, i.e., Left Battery of Left Group, and Right Battery of Right Group, will only fire Shrapnel and Smoke.

= 2 =

RATE OF FIRE - From Zero to Zero plus 24 - NORMAL.
From Zero plus 24 to Zero plus 84 SLOW.

(b) 4.5" HOWS.

4.5" How. batteries will open on a line 100 yards beyond 18-pdr. barrage and will lift back at this distance searching all trenches in their respective lanes until reaching barrage boundaries, when they will search back ceasing fire at Zero plus 84.
At Zero plus 84, 4.5" How. batteries will switch their lines of fire on to a line 500 yards South of the Northern Corps Boundary.

RATE OF FIRE - SLOW throughout.

The above barrage will be a flank barrage to the Canadian attack and a preparatory barrage for the advance Southwards of the 172nd Inf. Brigade.

4. SECOND BARRAGE.

This will open at Zero plus 90, 18-pdrs. on a line 200 yards South of the Corps Northern Boundary, 4.5" Hows. 500 yards South.
Brigades have been allotted equal portions from East to West.- 285th Brigade R.F.A., 9th Brigade R.F.A., 56th Bde. R.F.A., 5th Army Brigade R.F.A.

This barrage will consist of a Creeping Switch Barrage moving Southwards at the rate of 100 yards every 5 minutes until reaching the line HIPPO LANE - POSSUM LANE.
The greatest care must be taken by Battery Commanders that 18-pdrs. and Howitzers cannot shoot to the North (left) of the line on which this barrage opens.
4.5" Hows. will switch their fire to the right at same pace as 18-pdrs., but must keep 300 yards to the South (right) of the 18-pdr. Switch Barrage.
On reaching the line HIPPO LANE - POSSUM LANE, 4.5" Hows. will halt their fire on this line until Zero plus 120 when they will cease fire.
On reaching the line HIPPO LANE - POSSUM LANE, 18-pdrs. will cease fire at Zero plus 135 minutes.

AMMUNITION - 18-pdrs. Shrapnel only.

Rate of fire for both 18-pdrs. and 4.5" Hows. - NORMAL.

5. The 286th Brigade R.F.A. will advance at Zero plus 90 to the close support of 172nd Infantry Brigade. This Brigade will act directly under the orders of the G.O.C., 172nd Inf. Bde. to whom O.C., 286th Brigade R.F.A. should report for orders at Zero plus 80.

6. On the completion of the second barrage, Brigades must be prepared to advance without delay by Sections or Batteries to close support of 63rd Division which will pass through 57th Division.

7. Left Division Artillery will come under the orders of (A.G.O.C. 63rd Division when 63rd Division have passed through 57th Division. Command of Artillery will not change.

8. Left Heavy Artillery Group will act under the orders of B.G., Heavy Artillery, XVII Corps until Zero plus 135 minutes, when it reverts to Divisional control.

9. Orders for advance and action after Zero plus 135 minutes will be issued later.

Spare copy

S E C R E T.   To accompany XVII Corps No.G.(O)40

In connection with XVII Corps Order No.155.

Extracts from Canadian Corps Order No.234.
----

1.   The 1st Canadian Division will be attacking on the right of the Canadian Corps.

2.   The forming up line of the 1st Canadian Division will be approximately :-

   U.12.d.00. - U.12.b.central - V.1.a.central - P.31.central.

3.   1st Objective.

        CAGNICOURT - MOUNT DURY (P.27.b.) - DURY and high ground south of ETAING - joining northern boundary of XVII Corps about V.21.a.

        2nd Objective.

        The high ground in W.25.a. and 19.c. - the spur running N.E. through W.7.central and W.2.central - Q.33.central. - Q.22.a.

        3rd Objective.

        High Ground - E.4.central - through W.18.central - X.1 central - OISY-LE-VERGER in R.19.

        Any exploitation will then be carried out towards BOURLON WOOD and the PILGRIM'S REST (X.25.b.)

4.   The general idea of the operation is to break through the DROCOURT - QUEANT Line astride the CAMBRAI Road and then swing outwards rolling up the line to north and south.

5.   The advance from the 1st objective to the 2nd objective will be resumed at Zero plus 3 hours.

6.   Two companies of mark V tanks have been allotted to each Division attacking (24 fighting tanks).

7.   The barrage will come down 200 yards beyond the forming up line and remain for three minutes.
        Then 3 lifts of 100 yards each in 3 minutes and thence to 1st objective by lifts of 100 yards in 5 minutes.
        The protective barrage will be established beyond the RED Line until Zero plus 3 hours.

8.   Divisions will make special arrangements for mopping up trenches in the DROCOURT - QUEANT Line. It is suspected that this line contains several tunnels and, therefore, troops and tanks must be left to guard this line until all tunnels, etc. have been thoroughly mopped up.

H.Q. XVII Corps.   Sd. WALLACE WRIGHT, Brig.Genl.
1st Septr, 1918.   General Staff.

= 3 =

10. Every endeavour must be made by F.O.O's, Battery and Brigade Commanders to get information as to the situation through to Divisional Artillery as early as possible.

In an operation of this nature, its success must depend largely on accurate reports of the progress of the attack reaching Divisional Headquarters without delay.

Artillery F.O.O's can assist very materially. Every possible means of communication must be used and all previously tested.

C.W. Sets are being installed at U.19.d.8.6. and on high ground at U.1.a.

Messages can be sent by runner to from these stations, for transmission

11. NOTE TO 172ND INFANTRY BRIGADE.

172ND INFANTRY BRIGADE MUST NOT ADVANCE SOUTH OF THE NORTHERN CORPS BOUNDARY BEFORE ZERO PLUS 90, WHEN THE CREEPING SWITCH BARRAGE WILL OPEN.

12. Zero hour will be notified later.

13. Please acknowledge.

W E Pudkin.
Brigadier-General,
C.R.A., 57th Division.

Issued at 8 pm.

Copy No. 1/10. Right Group.
11/25. Left Group.
16/18. Left Heavy Artillery Group.
19/22. 172nd Infantry Brigade.
23. 57th Division "G".
24. XVII Corps R.A.
25. 63rd Divisional Artillery.
26. 40th Divisional Artillery.
27. 1st Canadian Artillery.
28. 57th Bn., M.G.C.
29. Staff Captain, R.A.
30. File.
31/32. War Diary.

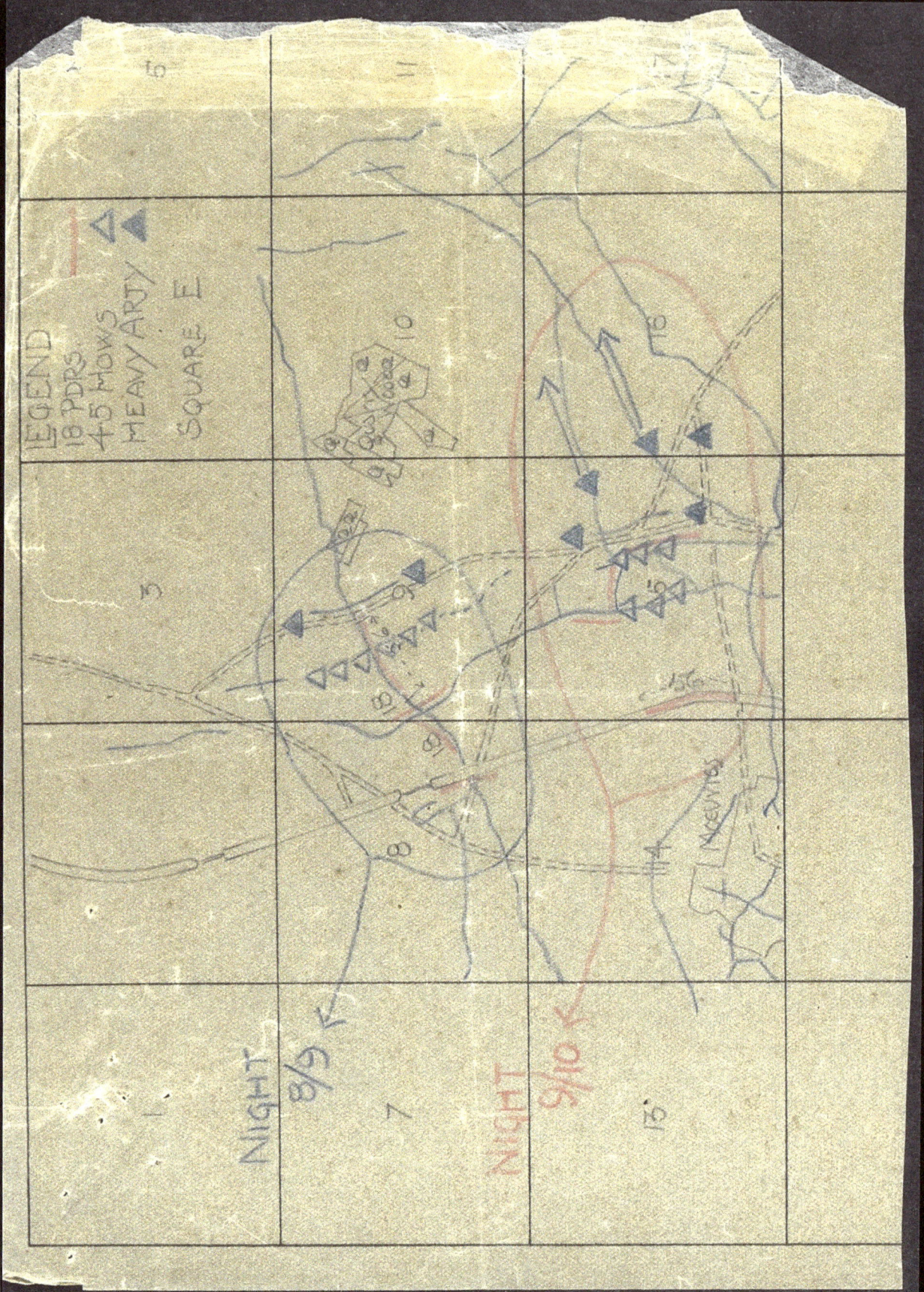

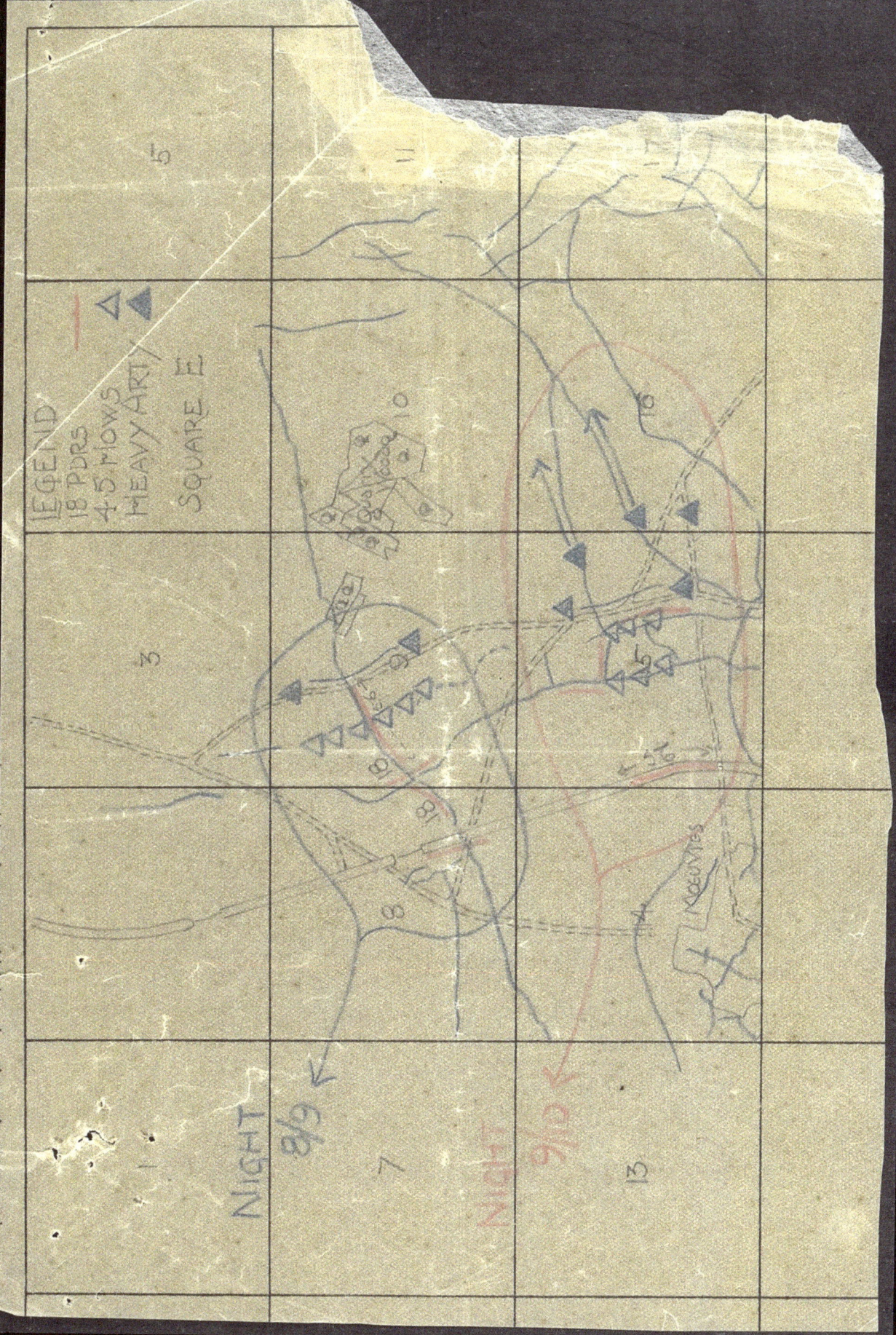

SKETCH 'B'

LEGEND
OUR DISPOSITIONS X
ENEMY DISPOSITIONS O
SQUARE E

SHELTER

HOBART

Identification Trace for

Map 'A'
S.O.S.
Lines
7.9.18

9th Bde
285 Bde
56th Bde

Section 286

LEGEND
18 Pdrs
4.5 hows △
NORTH &
SOUTH BOUNDARY
INTER ARTY BNDY -----

SECRET.　　　　　app III　　　　　52nd D.A. No. A/560.

9th Bde RFA.　5th Bde RFA.
56th Bde RFA.　285th Bde RFA.

1.　Attached tracing shows approximate line 9.0 am this morning and gives S.O.S. Lines and distribution between Brigades.
　　These Lines will come into force on receipt of this order.

2.　190 Brigade intend reaching the CANAL bank by a process of infiltration during the day and night.
　　When their advance comes too close to the S.O.S. Lines orders will be issued by this Office to lift S.O.S. Lines 200 yards.
　　The 18-pdr. S.O.S. Lines will then lift to a line 200 yards beyond and parallel to CANAL and 4.5" Howitzers will be 100 yards ahead of 18-prds. and on trenches etc when possible.

3.　Liaison will be as follows -
　　56th Brigade with 7th Fusiliers.
　　9th Brigade with ARTISTS RIFLES.
　　5th Brigade with 4th Bedfords.
　　Every effort to get close liaison and good communication must be made in order to give the Infantry the fullest support required during the process of infiltration.

4.　All movement in back areas to be fully sniped.

5.　Artillery Brigades to ACKNOWLEDGE.

　　　　　　　　　　　　　　　　[signature]
　　　　　　　　　　　　　　　　Captain R.A.
　　　　　　　　　　　Brigade Major R.A., 52nd D.A.
　　　　　　　　　　Left Group Artillery.

5th September 1919.

Copies to -
G.O.C. 190 Bde.) for information.
83rd D.A.　　　　)

NIGHT CONCENTRATIONS.
****

(To accompany 63rd (R.N.) D.A. Instructions No. 1.)

Date. Night.	Times.	Period.	Targets.
7/8th.	11.35 pm.	7 minutes.	(Tracks in QUARRY WOOD &
	1.55 am.	5 " "	(its Southern extension.
	4.15 am.	7 " "	(Road in G.10.a.
			(see photograph 13.LB.3561.
8/9th.	10.15 pm.	5 minutes.	Target Trench E9c 12.95 to E9a 71.43 To be fired by C 56
	1.0 am.	5 " "	A 56
	3.55 am.	7 " "	B 56 SEE MAP.
	5.55 am.	5 " "	C 56
9/10th.	8.45 pm.	5 minutes.	Fort CANAL DU NORD from E15a 05.05 to E15c 19.31 B 56
	11.10 pm.	7 " "	C 56
	1.25 am.	5 " "	A 56 SEE MAP.
	4.35 am.	5 " "	B 56

Rate of fire 2 rds per gun per minute

Rate of fire 2 rds per gun per minute

SECRET.   War Diary

63rd (R.N.) Divisional Artillery Instructions No.1.

7th September 1918.

The Corps policy is to worry the enemy as much as possible until we commence further offensive action.

Night concentrations will be fired, as shown on the attached pro-forma for the next three days, and should be carried out by one Battery per Brigade.

Gas will be used, where possible.

Combing barrages will be fired twice daily, on the lines arranged in 63rd (R.N.) Div.Arty.Operation Order No.266.

These barrages are in addition to day harassing fire, which O.C., Artillery Group will arrange with his Infantry Brigadier, and fire on opportunity targets.

In particular, the Canal Bank, especially the Western Bank, will be made as unhealthy as possible by enfilade fire from the Battery sited for that purpose.

J.C. Walford
Major R.A.,
Brigade Major,
63rd (R.N.) Divisional Artillery.

56 Bde RFA

Reference above
Please arrange to fire concentration
as ordered
Combing barrages are at present
in abeyance

A.H. Harris
Capt
Brigade Major
Left Group Arty

Ammunition.   9th and 56th Brigades.
         Creeping barrage - 50% A.   50% AX.
         Flanking barrage - 85% A.   15% AS.
         Smoke to be fired by left batteries of brigades only.
         286th Brigade on creeping barrage will fire smoke from its left battery.
         Ammunition for this brigade - 45% A. 40% AX. 15% AS.

Rates of fire.
         Zero to Zero plus 30 - NORMAL.
         Zero plus 30 to Zero plus 84 - SLOW.
         From Zero plus 84 to Zero plus 90 barrage forms on its Northern Line previous to switching.
         Zero plus 84 to Zero plus 135 - NORMAL.
         Howitzers stop at Zero plus 120.
         When Batteries reach the protective barrage they do not dwell on it but search communication and other trenches in their area until Zero plus 84.
         The flanking barrage halts on POSSUM and HIPPO LANES.
         ZERO HOUR will be 5.0 A.M.
         Howitzers in creeping barrage should jump from trench to trench as the 18-pdr. barrage comes up to the trench.
         In the flanking barrage the howitzers will keep 300 yards South of the 18-pdr. barrage and will stop at Zero plus 120.
         The creeping barrage will remain on the opening line till Zero plus 10 and will then creep forward at 100 yards per 3 minutes till Zero plus 19 after which it moves 100 yards forward every 5 minutes until it reaches protective line.
         From Zero plus 90 to Zero plus 135 the barrage will move to the right i.e., south, at the rate of 100 yards per 5 minutes.
         Batteries should be ready to move from Zero plus 2 hours 30 minutes with full Echelons.

SECRET. 52nd D.A. No. A/565.

9th Brigade RFA.
56th Brigade RFA.
285th Brigade RFA.
============================

    286th Brigade is not now coming into the line.
    The Group will remain as at present constituted.
    S.O.S. Lines will be as on attached tracing, which also shows North and South boundaries and inter-Artillery Brigade boundaries for **harassing fire**.

    Liaison will be as under.-
9th Brigade RFA with Bedfords.
56th Brigade RFA with ARTISTS RIFLES.

    The relief of the 9th Brigade Liaison Officer with ARTISTS by 56th Brigade RFA and of 285th Brigade RFA Liaison Officer with Bedfords by 9th Brigade RFA will be mutually arranged between Brigades concerned, but outgoing Liaison Officer must remain till incoming Liaison Officer has got communication with his Brigade.

    Brigades to ACKNOWLEDGE.

                                                    Captain R.A.
                                     Brigade Major R.A., 52nd D.A.
                                        LEFT GROUP ARTILLERY.

6th September 1918.
Copies to -
            190th Infantry Brigade.
            63rd Divisional Arty.

SECRET

52nd D.A. No. A/560/1.

APP. IV

9th Bde RFA.
56th Bde RFA.
285th Bde RFA.

Consequent upon 5th Bde RFA being withdrawn and a change in holding our line, amendments will be made to my No. A/560.
S.O.S. lines will be as shown on attached tracing.
Liaison will be as under.
56th Bde RFA with Fusiliers.
9th Bde RFA with ARTISTS RIFLES.
285th Bde RFA with Bedfords.
285th Bde RFA will relieve the 5th Bde RFA with Bedfords at once.
Zones for harassing fire for Brigades will be -
9th Bde RFA - E and W grid between E.9. & E.15 to E & W grid between E.2. & E.3.
56th Bde RFA - Southern boundary to E & W grid between E.9. & E.15.
285th Bde RFA - E & W grid between E.2. & E.3 to Northern boundary.

Artillery Bdes to ACKNOWLEDGE.

Captain R.A.
Brigade Major R.A., 52nd DA.
LEFT GROUP ARTILLERY.

5th September 1918.
Copies to -
5th Bde RFA.
63rd Div'l Arty.
G.O.C. 190 Bde.

App VII

9" Bde

285 Bde

56" Bde

Legend

18/odrs ———
H.G hows △
NORTH &
SOUTH boundary
inter arty bdy

E

Legend
18 hrs —
4.5 hrs △

aps.

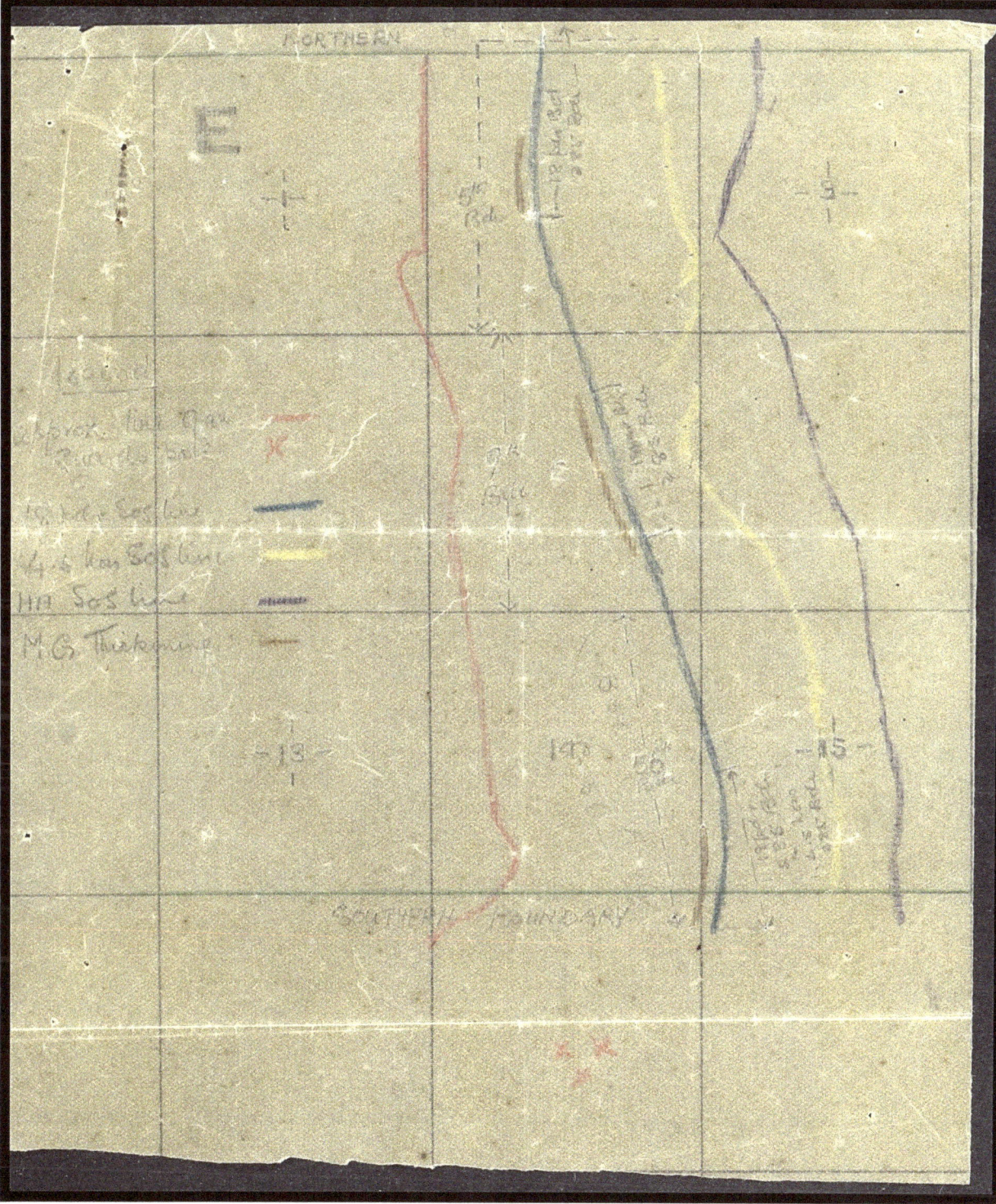

NOTE.—(1). These traces are intended to facilitate the communication of information as to the position of targets, which have be
(2). The squares on this trace are 500 yards in length on the 1/10,000 scale, 1,000 yards in length on the 1/20,000 sc on the 1/40,000 scale.
(3). The squares on the trace are fitted to the squares of the map showing the targets, which are then draw letters and numbers must also be added to enable the recipient to place the trace in the correct position on his may also be traced, but this is not essential. The name and scale of the map to which the trace refers must b can be used for the 1/10,000, 1/20,000, or 1/40,000 scale.

G.S.G.S. 3023.

"A" Form.
MESSAGES AND SIGNALS.

Prefix	Code	Words	Charge	This message is on a/c of:	Recd. at m.
Office of Origin and Service Instructions.		Sent			Date
		At m.		Service	From
		To			
		By		(Signature of "Franking Officer.")	By

TO: 9th Bde
56 Bde ✓
285 Bde

Sender's Number.	Day of Month.	In reply to Number.	AAA
F 97	7		

reference attached aaa 9th Bde will take Northern Zone aaa 285 Bde Centre Zone aaa 56 Bde Southern Zone aaa Zero hour for this evenings barrage will be 5.30 pm aaa acknowledge

4 30

From
Place: Left Group
Time

(Z) W Harris?

SECRET.   52nd D.A. No. A/567.

App VII

9th Brigade RFA.
56th Brigade RFA.
285th Brigade RFA.
===================

  Attached tracing 'A' gives new S.O.S. Lines that will come into force upon receipt of this.

2. Tracing 'B' is a rough sketch of our and enemy disposition.

3. The following is information obtained from sketch found on dead Company Commander, 1st Coy. 187 I.R., 187 Division killed night 6/7th giving disposition of his Company for that night.

(i) OUTPOST LINE.
Sunken Road E.8.a.8.6. to 65.00. with L.M.G. Posts at E.8.a.8.6., E.8.a.75.40., E.8.a.65.00.

(ii) MAIN LINE.
West bank of CANAL from light railway at E.8.b.05.95. to Bridge at E.8.b.3.4. inclusive with L.M.G. Posts at E.8.b.05.95., E.8.b.15.75., E.8.b.3.4.

(iii) ROUTE FOR RELIEF.
Via HOBART STREET passed Regtl. H.Qrs. (not marked) to lock 4. Troops relieved to go out via trench E.8.d.85.65.

(iv) The above sketch was made by an N.C.O. of the Coy. concerned. Sent forward to reconnoitre.

(v) There is some splinter proof cover in CANAL for M.G. crews.

              Captain R.A,
           Brigade Major R.A., 52nd D.A.
            LEFT GROUP ARTILLERY.

7th September 1918.

Copies to -
  63rd D.A.
  190 Inf. Bde.

"C" Form.
MESSAGES AND SIGNALS.

Army Form C. 2123.
(In books of 100.)
No. of Message App VIII

| Prefix SB | Code FA | Words 34 | Received. From ZA By JNO | Sent or sent out. At ___ m. To ___ By ___ | Office Stamp. RA 7/9/18 6.15 pm |

Service Instructions ZA Pty

Handed in at ___ Office ___ m. Received 6.15 pm

TO SERA

Sender's Number	Day of Month.	In reply to Number	AAA
F99	7/9		

Reconnoitre and move up 2 guns from your brigade as far up as you consider possible tonight aaa these guns are intended for use in cropping back areas

FROM
PLACE & TIME   Left Group

app× XI

56th. Brigade, No. R.14.

All Bde. Batteries.
==================

       Brigade zone is that bounded on North by East and West grid line between E 10 and E 14, and on South by East and West grid line between E 14 a. and E 14 d.
       H.F. to-night ----- 100 rds. per Battery over this area from S.O.S. Line eastwards, special attention being paid to CANAL DU NORD LINE.

    Times of firing.-

    A Battery.....................10 pm to 11 pm.

    B Battery.....................11pm to 12 midnight.

    C Battery..................... 3 am to 4 am.

    527 Battery................... 4 am to 5 am.

    ACKNOWLEDGE.

                                Captain, R.F.A.
                       Adjutant, 56th. Brigade. R.F.A

6th. September, 1918.

56th. Brigade No R.15

All Bde. Batteries.
==================

       The 63rd. (R.N.) Division is being relieved by the 57th. Division on 7/8th. September 1918.

       Location of Divisional and D.A. Headquarters will be notified later.

                                Captain, R.F.A.
                       Adjutant, 56th. Brigade, R.F.A.

6th. September, 1918.

52nd D.A. No. A/570.

SECRET.

9th Bde RFA.
56th Bde RFA.
285th Bde Sub-group.

286th Bde RFA has now come into the line and with 285th Bde RFA has been formed into a Sub-group.

Liaison arrangements will now be as follows :-

56th Bde RFA with Right Battalion.
285th Bde RFA Sub-group with Left Battalion.

9th Bde RFA will now become a silent brigade and will only fire in the case of S.O.S.
They will however keep all communications with O.Ps etc. down and will arrange to test them once daily.

S.O.S. lines will be as in the attached tracing, the fire of the 9th Bde batteries being superimposed on that of batteries of a similar nature, in the zones allotted to them.
These S.O.S. lines will come into force at 6.0 pm this evening.

Captain R.A.
Brigade Major R.A., 52nd D.A. Group

8th September 1918.

Copies to -
    171st Infantry Brigade.) for information.
    57th Divisional Arty.)

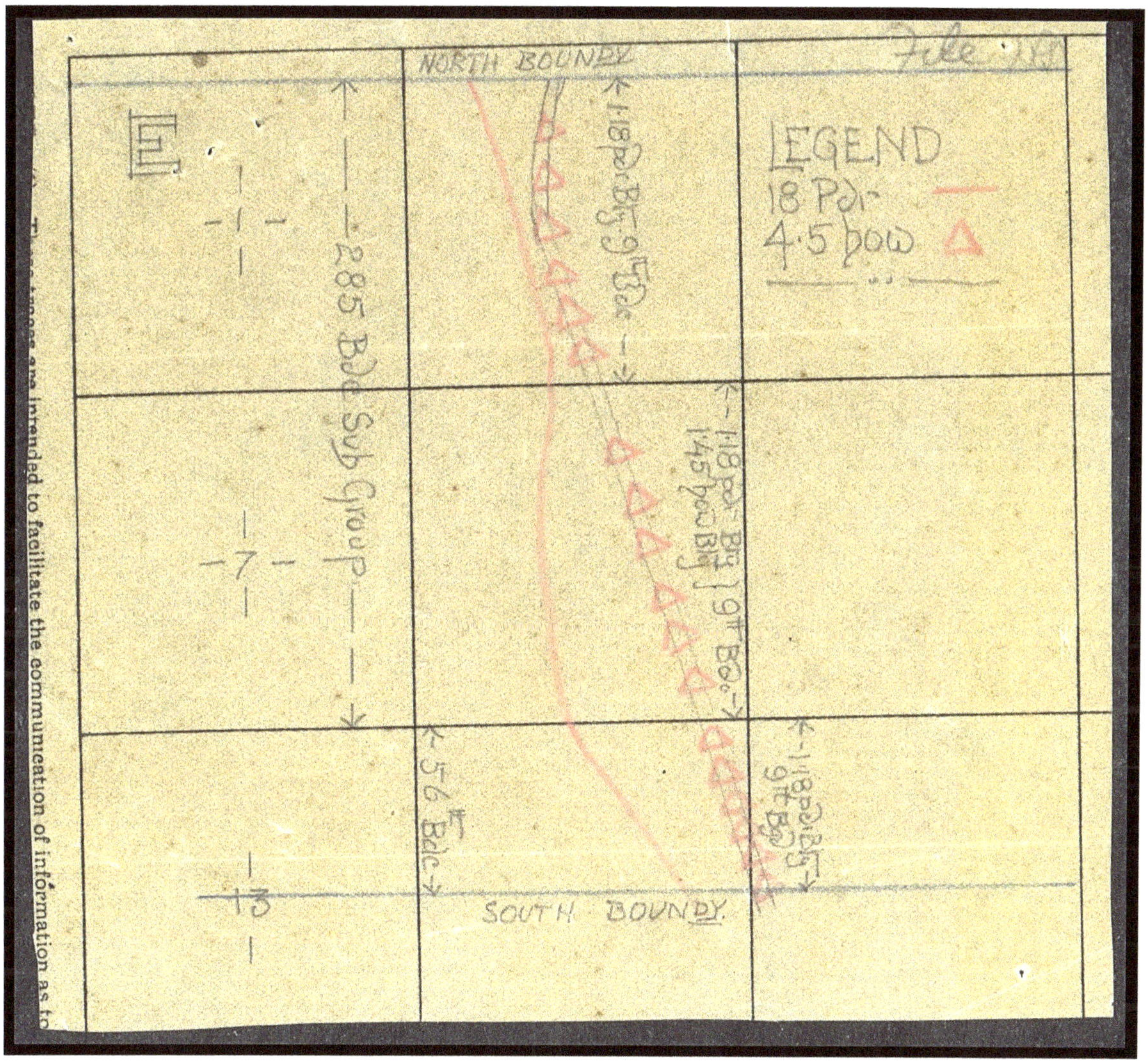

NORTH BOUNDY

File ...

LEGEND
18 Pdr —
4.5 how △

E

←—— 285 Bde Sub Group ——→

←118 Pdr Bty 9th Bde

←118 pdr Bty | 9th Bde→
145 how Bty

←56 Bde

←118 Pdr Bty
9th Bde

SOUTH BOUNDY

Legend

Right Battalion unit
will be at 8·0 p.m.
tonight as reported by
Liaison Officer

Guards have been asked
to establish this Post

Left Post of Irish Guards

Suspected Enemy Posts

Enemy M.G.

"C" FORM.
MESSAGES AND SIGNALS.

Army Form C. 2123.
(In books of 100.)

No. of Message ....

| Prefix... M | Code..... | Words... 91 | Received. From 7 D By SW71 | Sent, or sent out. At .... m. To .... By .... | Office Stamp. RA 9/9/18 |

Service Instructions: F/EB   Tele W.T

Handed in at .... Office .... m. Received 10.1.00 m.

TO Rra

*Sender's Number. 1708	Day of Month. 9	In reply to Number.	AAA
Ref	63 DA	order	No 226 aaa
5&6 Bde	will	fire	creeper
on southern	zone	at 1 am
aaa 2&5 Bde	will	fire
creeper	on	centre	zone
at	4 am	10th instead	rate
of	fire	will	be
1 rd	per	gun per	minute
and	lifts	100 yds per
minute and	not	as
stated	in	the	order
aaa	Added	5&6 2&5 Bdes
reptd	57 DA

FROM PLACE & TIME Left Group

SECRET.
****

CO XIII

D.A. 32/186.

Copy No. 6

57th Divisional Artillery Order No. 63.

16/September/1918.

1. The 57th Divisional Artillery will be relieved in the line tonight the 16th instant by the 40th Divisional Artillery.

2. 178th Brigade R.F.A. will relieve 285th Brigade R.F.A.
   181st Brigade R.F.A. will relieve 286th Brigade R.F.A.

3. Battery reliefs will be carried out by Sections.

4. Brigades, on relief, will proceed to their respective Wagon Lines.

5. Details of relief will be arranged by Brigade Commanders concerned.

6. Command of Groups will pass on completion of relief, and R.A.H.Q. notified by wire. Code Word "COMPLETE".

7. All ammunition in Battery Positions of 57th Div. Arty. will be taken on charge by incoming units. Staff Captain R.A. will be notified by wire the amounts handed over.

8. The responsibility for supply of ammunition by 57th D.A.C. will cease at midnight 16th/17th instant.

9. Arrangements for relief of 57th Trench Mortar Batteries at a future date will be issued separately.

10. The 57th Divisional Artillery (less D.A.C. and T.M. Batteries) will move to the BOIRY - HENIN area tomorrow the 17th instant; details of route will be issued later.

11. Artillery units please acknowledge.

C.T.Baynham
Major,
a/Brigade Major, R.A.,
57th Division.

Issued at 12 noon.

Copy No. 1. 285th Brigade R.F.A.
       2. 286th Brigade R.F.A.
       3. 178th Brigade R.F.A.
       4. 181st Brigade R.F.A.
       5. 9th Brigade R.F.A.
       6. 56th Brigade R.F.A.
       7. 57th D.T.M.O.
       8. 57th Div. Ammn. Col.
       9. XVII Corps R.A.
      10. 57th Division "G".

No. 11. 57th Division "Q"
    12. 52nd Div. Arty.
    13. Staff Captain R.A.
    14. Signal Officer, R.A.
    15. 62nd Brigade R.G.A.
    16. XVII Corps H.A.
    17. Guards Div. Arty.
    18. 1st Can. Div. Arty.
    19. File.
  20/21. War Diary.

Identification Trace for use with Artillery Maps.

E Northern zone →

Centre zone → ZERO LINE

Southern zone → S Boundary →

SECRET.

63RD (R.N.) DIVISIONAL ARTILLERY OPERATION ORDER No.226.
****

7th September 1918.

1. Under instructions received from XVII Corps R.A., the following programme of artillery work will be carried out until further orders.

2. A combing barrage will be fired twice a day by 18 pdrs. and 4.5" Howrs., in accordance with trace attached.

(a) 18 pounders.

(i) Northern Zone. At ZERO, the barrage will be opened for two minutes along the western bank of the CANAL DU NORD and will move forward in 100 yard lifts every two minutes until the RED Line (see tracing) is reached.
When this line is reached, the barrage will cease fire.
At ZERO plus 16 mins. it will lift on to the DOTTED RED Line in E.4.a & c. and will again move forward at the same rate and pace until the line of M.G.posts East of the MARQUION Line is reached.(BLUE Line)

(ii) Centre Zone. At ZERO, the barrage will be opened for two minutes along the Western bank of the CANAL DU NORD and will move forward continuously until the BLUE Line is reached.

(iii) Southern Zone. At ZERO, the barrage will open on the Western bank of the CANAL DU NORD for two minutes and will move forward to the Sunken Road in E.15.b & d. (RED Line) and cease fire.
At ZERO plus 16 mins. it will lift to the DOTTED RED Line and again move forward to the BLUE Line.

3. As soon as fire has reached the BLUE Line in each zone, the barrage will be brought back at the same rate and pace until the line of the CANAL DU NORD is reached again, when fire will cease.

4. 4.5" Howitzers.

(i) Northern Zone. 4.5" Hows. will open on a line 300 yards East of the 18 pdrs. and move forward at the same pace, maintaining the same distance from the 18 pdr.barrage.

(ii) Centre Zone. 4.5" Hows. will open on the trench in E.8.b. and E.9.c. As soon as the 18 pdr.barrage has reached this trench, they will lift to Sunken Road running through E.9.central and remain on it until the 18 pdrs. reach the Sunken Road, when they will lift on to QUARRY WOOD and the Wood West of it in E.9.b.cent., until the 18 pdrs. reach the BLUE Line, when they will be brought back on to the Sunken Road in E.9.central.

(iii) Southern Zone. 4.5" Hows. open on the Sunken Road, E.15. b & d. for two minutes, and will then move up by successive lifts of 100 yards along HEIDER Trench, THREX Street, EDWARD Street, until the MARQUION Line is reached, when they will bombard M.G. posts in E.11.c., E.17.a. for two minutes, when fire will be lifted straight back to the trenches in E.15.b & d.

- 2 -

5. 4.5" Hows. will, in the Northern Zone conform to the 18 pdrs., in the Centre and Southern Zones cease fire at the same time as the 18 pdrs.

6. Rate :- 1 round per gun and howr. per minute.
   Pace:- 100 yards every two minutes.
   Ammunition :- 50% "A", 50% "AX".
   4.5" Hows: No.106 fuze.

7. Time for today's barrage will be notified later. Tomorrow, 8th instant, 5.15 a.m.

8. Artillery Brigades please acknowledge.

J. C. Walford
Major R.A.,
Brigade Major,
63rd (R.N.) Divisional Artillery.

7th September 1918.

Appendix 11

SECRET.

D.A. 7/489.

57th Divisional Artillery Order No. 61.

1. The 285th and 56th Brigades R.F.A. will be required to fire a Smoke Barrage on the afternoon of the 11th instant, and again on the morning of the 12th instant.

2. The purpose of the barrage will be to form a screen on approximately the line E.17.c.0.0. - E.18.d.5.0. to prevent observation from the high ground in E.17.a. & b. and E.18.a.

3. The following batteries will be employed :-

   <u>285TH BRIGADE R.F.A.</u> - 3 18-pdr. batteries, 1 4.5" How. Bty.

   <u>56TH BRIGADE R.F.A.</u> - 2 18-pdr. batteries, 1 4.5" How. Bty.

4. Ammunition as stated below will be available at C.3.a.5.5. at 5 pm. tomorrow the 10th instant. Brigades will arrange to draw at following times :-

      285th Brigade R.F.A.   5 pm.
      56th Brigade R.F.A.   6.30 pm.

   Ammunition will be taken straight to Battery positions-

   Each 18-pdr. Battery   -   500 AS.
      " 4.5" How. Battery -   250 BS.

5. Details of the Barrage will be issued later.

6. Brigades please acknowledge. done 0195

                                          Major,
                                 a/Brigade Major, R.A.,
                                       57th Division.

9/September/1918.

Copy to - 285th Brigade R.F.A.
          56th Brigade R.F.A.
          52nd Div. Arty.   )
          Staff Capt. R.A.) for information.

          A & B 527

Received
12.5 pm.
10/9/18

SECRET.

56th. Brigade No. R.117.

A/56 Battery.
C/56 Battery.
527 How.Battery.
==================

Reference 57th.Divisional Artillery Order No.61 dated 9/9/18.

1. The 57th.Divisional Artillery will co-operate in two operations carried out by the VI Corps on September 11th. and 12th. by placing a Smoke Barrage to deny observation from area E.17. - E.18. to the S.W.

2. The Smoke screen will be put down by Brigades already detailed from zero minus 2 minutes to zero plus 50 minutes.

3. Ammunition available for each operation.-

    Each 18 Pdr.Battery............250 rds. "AS"
    Each 4.5 How.Battery..........125 rds. "BS"

4. Tasks as under.-
    A/56 Battery E.17.c.0.0. to E.17.c.75.00.
    C/56 Battery E.17.c.75.00. to E.17.d.50.00.
    527 How.Bty. E.17.c.0.0. to E.17.d.5.0.

5. The attached notes on the employment of Smoke Shell are issued for guidance.
   The rates of fire will be adjusted according to the ammunition available"

6. The area on which the shell will be fired to obtain the screening effect will necessarily depend upon the wind previous to zero hour. B.C's will give this their careful consideration.
   A salvo will be fired by all guns at zero minus 2 minutes.

7. Zero hour on each day will be notified later.

8. Batteries to ACKNOWLEDGE by wire.

                                        Captain, R.F.A.
                                Adjutant, 56th.Brigade R.F.A.

11th.September, 1918

SECRET.
*****

W Diary

Received 8.40 am
11/9/18

D.A. 7/492.
Copy No. 1.

57th Divisional Artillery Operation Order No. 35.

10/September/1918.

Reference 57th Divisional Artillery Order No. 61, dated 9/9/18.

1. The 57th Divisional Artillery will co-operate in two Operations carried out by the VI Corps on September 11th and 12th by placing a Smoke Barrage to deny observation from area E.17. - E.18. to the S.W.

2. The Smoke Screen will be put down by Brigades already detailed from Zero minus 2 minutes to Zero plus 50 minutes.

3. Ammunition available for each Operation :-

   Each 18-pdr. Battery   -   250 rounds AS.
   Each 4.5" How. Battery -   125 rounds BS.

4. Brigade Zones are allotted as follows :-

   56th Brigade R.F.A. - E.17.c.0.0. to E.17.d.5.0.
   285th Brigade R.F.A. - E.17.d.5.0. to E.18.d.6.0.

5. The attached notes on the employment of Smoke shell are issued for guidance.
   The rates of fire will be adjusted according to the ammunition available.

6. The area on which the shell will be fired to obtain the screening effect will necessarily depend upon the wind previous to Zero hour. Brigade Commanders will give this their careful consideration.
   A salvo will be fired by all guns at Zero minus 2 minutes.

7. Zero hour on each day will be notified later.

8. Brigades please acknowledge. done 02.06.

C.T.Baynham.
Major,
a/Brigade Major, R.A.,
57th Division.

Issued at 3 pm.

Copy No. 1. Right Group.
         2. Left Group.
         3. 57th Division "G"
         4. XVII Corps R.A.
         5. 62nd Brigade R.G.A.
         6. Staff Captain, R.A.
         7. 170th Infantry Brigade.
         8. 171st Infantry Brigade.
         9. 172nd Infantry Brigade.
        10. File.
     11/12. War Diary.

No 117/1   3rd Brigade A159
                        11th Regiment r 198

Cols A/36 C/36 + 5.7 Bty.

Reference my R117 of date.
Zero hour for the joint operation
tomorrow morning (17th inst.) will
be 3.25 am.

Periods for simple screen
will be Zero to Zero plus 10,
Zero plus 80 to Zero plus 180.

If sufficient ammunition
is available, smoke screen
will be continued from Zero plus 10 to
Zero plus 80. The most important
period is from Zero plus 65
to Zero plus 180.

Acknowledge by wire.

                    R S Waller
14/9/18   A/Lt 46 Sept.

SECRET.

D.A. 7/493.

Copy No. 6

Appendix 10

57th Divisional Artillery Operation Order No. 36.

11/September/1918.

1. In conjunction with an Operation by the VI Corps on our right, the 57th Division will capture the line of the Canal on the Divisional front, and afterwards exploit enemy trench line as far as the following points :- E.9.c.10.90. - E.15.b.30.00. - E.15.d.35.20. - E.21.b.30.85.

2. 170th Infantry Brigade will attack on their Brigade front on the right; 171st Infantry Brigade on their Brigade front on the left.   Forming up line for Infantry -

   Right (170th) Brigade - E.19.d.55.00. - E.19.d.55.35. - E.20.a.00.20.
   - E.14.c.00.50. - E.14.a.40.00.

   Left (171st) Brigade - E.14.a.40.00. - along the line of the
   Railway to E.8.a.25.35. - E.2.c.0.0. -
   W.26.c.0.0.

3. The attack will be made under 18-pdr. Creeping Barrage supported by 4.5" and 6" Hows.
   Zero hour will be 6.15 pm. this evening.

4. ORDERS FOR 18-PDR. BARRAGE.

   Opening barrage line will be :- E.20.c.10.00. - E.20.a.38.00.
   - E.14.c.35.12. - E.14.a.80.00. (RIGHT GROUP).
   E.14.a.80.00. - E.8.c.60.00. - E.2.c.55.00. - E.2.c.60.77. -
   E.2.a.75.80. (LEFT GROUP.)

   Batteries forming 18-pdr. Barrage for RIGHT GROUP will be -

         56th Brigade R.F.A. - 3 Batteries.
         9th Brigade R.F.A. - 2 Batteries.
         178th Brigade R.F.A. - 3 Batteries.

   Batteries forming 18-pdr. Barrage for Left Group will be -

         295th Brigade R.F.A. - 3 Batteries.
         286th Brigade R.F.A. - 2 Batteries.
         9th Brigade R.F.A. - 1 Battery.
         181st Brigade R.F.A. - 2 Batteries.

   Lanes of fire for Batteries will, in all cases, be from West to East parallel to Grid Line.

   Barrage will remain on opening line for 4 minutes and will then creep back at the rate of 100 yards every 5 minutes until reaching the following line :-

   W.26.d.60.00. - E.8.b.90.25. - thence along the trench line to E.21.a.95.95. - thence to E.21.c.30.00.   Here the barrage will remain for 15 minutes.

= 2 =

The following batteries of Left Group will then cease fire -

286TH BRIGADE R.F.A. -
   286th Brigade R.F.A.
    9th Brigade R.F.A. 1 Battery.
   181st Brigade R.F.A.

The 3 Batteries of 285th Brigade R.F.A. will then form a Box Barrage as follows :-

E.9.a.00.50. - E.9.a.50.20. - E.9.c.85.50. - E.9.c.50.40.

This Box Barrage will remain on until 8.15 pm.

ACTION OF RIGHT GROUP BATTERIES.

After forming Protector Barrage as above for 15 minutes, barrage will creep forward in lifts as before (100 yards every 5 minutes) until reaching N. and S. line E.16.a.0.0. - E.22.c.0.0. On reaching this line, one 18-pdr., 56th Brigade R.F.A. will enfilade trench from E.15.d.55.10. to E.22.a.40.90., one 18-pdr. 56th Brigade R.F.A. will enfilade trench from E.21.b.50.77. to E.22.a.30.53., one 18-pdr. 56th Brigade R.F.A. will search and sweep Round trench in E.21.b. & d.
  These 3 batteries will cease fire at 8.15 pm.
  All other batteries of Right Group will cease fire after 15 minutes on the Protector Line.

ACTION FOR 4 GUNS, A/286 enfilading Canal -

These guns will, from Zero to Zero plus 15, enfilade the Canal from E.2.d.20.00. to E.8.d.80.00. SHRAPNEL ONLY.
Care must be taken that they do not shoot North of former point.
RATE OF FIRE - Zero to Zero plus 5 - RAPID.
     Zero plus 5 to Zero plus 15. NORMAL.

Ammunition and Rates of fire for 18-pdr. batteries in Creeping Barrage will be as follows :-

AMMUNITION. 50% H.E., 50% Shrapnel.

Those batteries which have Smoke Shell will fire 10% Smoke up to Zero plus 50.

RATES OF FIRE - Zero to Zero plus 4 - INTENSE.
    Zero plus 4 until reach Protector Line NORMAL,
     with the exception that 2 batteries 9th Brigade
     R.F.A., RIGHT GROUP, will continue at RAPID rate
     until the Protector barrage.

ACTION FOR 4.5" HOWS.

RIGHT GROUP. 9th Brigade How. Battery :-

2 Hows. - Zero to Zero plus 10 - Enemy Work E.14.d.55.10.
  Zero plus 10 to Zero plus 20 - Road across Canal
   E.15.c.20.30.
  Zero plus 20 to Zero plus 30 - Trench, E.15.d.03.65.
  Zero plus 30 to Zero plus 90 - Search up EDWARD STREET
   from E.16.a.00.00. to E.16.b.30.75.

= 3 =

2 Hows. - Zero to Zero plus 6 - E.20.a.90.80.
       Zero plus 6 to Zero plus 20 - Search down Trench from
         E.20.a.90.80. to E.21.a.00.60.
       Zero plus 20 to Zero plus 30 - Lock No. 5 in E.21.a.
       Zero plus 30 to Zero plus 90 - LYNX SUPPORT from
         E.16.c.00.00. to E.22.b.00.80.

2 Hows. - Zero to Zero plus 5 - E.20.a.95.50.
       Zero plus 5 to Zero plus 15 - E.20.b.65.25.
       Zero plus 15 to Zero plus 30 - Search down LYNX TRENCH
         from E.21.a.15.60. to E.21.a.95.95.
       Zero plus 30 to Zero plus 90 - LYNX TRENCH from E.21.b.80.60.
         to E.22.a.45.55.

  1 How. Battery, 178th Brigade R.F.A.

2 Hows. - Zero to Zero plus 5 - E.20.d.40.70.
       Zero plus 5 to Zero plus 10 - E.20.d.90.65.
       Zero plus 10 to Zero plus 90 - ROUND TRENCH, E.21.b. & d.

2 Hows. - Zero to Zero plus 5 - E.20.c.80.80.
       Zero plus 5 to Zero plus 12 - Searching trench, thence to
         Canal at E.20.d.90.65.
       Zero plus 12 to Zero plus 90 - Sunken Road from E.21.c.25.55.
         to E.21.d.00.20.

2 Hows. - Zero to Zero plus 4 - E.20.c.60.20.
       Zero plus 4 to Zero plus 15 - Searching down trench, thence
         to Canal.
       Zero plus 15 to Zero plus 60 - Area about ROUND TRENCH.

RIGHT GROUP HOWS.

D/286. 2 Hows. - Zero to Zero plus 5 - On hedge from E.8.b.10.95.
             to E.8.a.80.60.

       4 Hows. - Enemy Work about E.8.d.25.75.

       Above hows. at Zero plus 5 and Zero plus 12 respectively will
lift to line of dugouts and Sunken Road in E.3.a. & c. sweeping them
until Zero plus 40.
             Zero plus 40 to Zero plus 90 - Sunken Road in E.9.a.
               and HOBART TRENCH in E.9.b. and E.10.a., searching.

D/181. 2 Hows. - Zero to Zero plus 10 - Searching down HOBART STREET
             from E.8.d.00.20. to its junction with Canal.
           Zero plus 10 to Zero plus 90 - Area about E.9.b.cent.

       4 Hows. - Zero to Zero plus 15 - Sweeping Canal in E.8.d. and
             E.14.b.
           Zero plus 15 to Zero plus 25 - CANAL DU NORD Line in
             E.9.c. and E.15.a.
           Zero plus 25 to Zero plus 90 - QUARRY WOOD and its
             approaches.

RATES OF FIRE, 4.5" HOW BATTERIES -

       Zero to Zero plus 5   -   RAPID.
       Zero plus 5 to Zero plus 30   NORMAL.
       Afterwards   -   SLOW.

     4.5" How. Batteries must not shoot within 200 yards of
Creeping Barrage.

= 4 =

6" HOW. BATTERIES.

Zero to Zero plus 30 - One 6" How. Battery LYNX TRENCH E.21.b.00.95. to E.22.a.00.55.
One 6" How. Battery LYNX SUPPORT Trench E.15.d.00.25. to E.16.c.00.90.

Zero plus 30 to Zero plus 90 - One 6" How. Battery QUARRY WOOD and its approaches, E.10.a. & c.
One 6" How. Battery LYNX TRENCH from E.22.b.00.20. to E.22.d.00.00.

RATES OF FIRE, 6" HOWS.

Zero to Zero plus 30   -   NORMAL.
Zero plus 30 to Zero plus 90   SLOW.

5.   2nd Canadian Artillery on left will co-operate as follows :-

From Zero to Zero plus 45 - Shrapnel Barrage on SAINS-LEZ-MARQUION, and with 4.5" How. Battery on houses on Canal at W.26.d.00.30.

6.   A Contact aeroplane will call for flares at 7.30 pm. and at 8 pm.

7.   Watches will be synchronised at 170th and 171st Infantry Brigades Headquarters at 4 pm. to-day.

8.   ACKNOWLEDGE.

Issued at 2.15 pm.

Brigadier-General,
C.R.A., 57th Division.

Copy No. 1/5.   9th Brigade R.F.A.
       6/10.   56th Brigade R.F.A.
      11/15.   178th Brigade R.F.A.
      16/19.   181st Brigade R.F.A.
      20/24.   285th Brigade R.F.A.
      25/29.   286th Brigade R.F.A.
      30/32.   170th Infantry Brigade.
      33/36.   171st Infantry Brigade.
         37.   57th Division "G"
         38.   XVII Corps R.A.
         39.   2nd Canadian Artillery.
         40.   52nd Div. Arty.
         41.   Guards Div. Arty.
         42.   57th Bn., M.G.C.
         43.   XVII Corps H.A.
         44.   File.
      45/46.   War Diary.

SECRET.

D.A. 7/494.
Copy No...1...

57th Divisional Artillery Operation Order No. 37.

11/September/1918.

1. Reference 57th Divisional Artillery Operation Order No. 35 of the 10th September, 1918.

2. Zero hour for the main Operation tomorrow morning will be 5.25 am.

3. Periods for Smoke Screen will be :-

Zero to Zero plus 10.
Zero plus 80 to Zero plus 180.

4. It will be observed that a pause has been made from Zero plus 10 to Zero plus 80.
If sufficient ammunition is available, the Smoke Screen will be continued during this period also.
The most important period is From Zero plus 80 to Zero plus 180.

                                                  for Major,
                                         a/Brigade Major, R.A.,
Issued at 4.30 pm.   57th Division.

Copy No. 1. Right Group.
        2. Left Group.
        3. 57th Division "G".
        4. XVII Corps R.A.
        5. 62nd Brigade R.G.A.
        6. Staff Captain, R.A.
        7. 170th Infantry Brigade.
        8. 171st Infantry Brigade.
        9. 172nd Infantry Brigade.
     10. File.
  11/12. War Diary.

NOTES ON EMPLOYMENT OF SMOKE SHELL.

1. **18-PDR. Q.F. SHELL, FILLED W.P.**

    In warm dry, sunny weather, with a wind of very low velocity (drift 5 miles per hour) blowing on to objective and along the line of fire -

    (i) One gun will cover 15 yards of front.

    (ii) A continuous barrage can be established and maintained over a given front by firing a salvo followed by Battery Fire 2 secs., in other words, once the cloud is established by a salvo every 15 yards of front should receive 5 rounds per minute to ensure a continuous barrage.
    Experiment shows that this is best done by Battery Fire and not by firing Salvos.

    4.5" HOW. SHELL, FILLED W.P.

    With wind blowing on to objective one gun will cover 20 yards of front. A continuous barrage can be established and maintained over a given front by firing a salvo followed by Battery Fire, 10 secs., i.e., every 30 yards of front should receive 1 round per minute.

2. Should the wind be blowing down the target -

    18-pdr. Battery will cover 150 yards of front.

    4.5" How. Battery will cover 800 yards of front.

    The same rate being employed as above.

****

NOTES ON EMPLOYMENT OF SMOKE SHELL.
****

1. 18-PDR. Q.F. SHELL, FILLED W.P.

    In warm dry, sunny weather, with a wind of very low velocity (drift 5 miles per hour) blowing on to objective and along the line of fire -

    (i) One gun will cover 15 yards of front.

    (ii) A continuous barrage can be established and maintained over a given front by firing a salvo followed by Battery Fire 2 secs., in other words, once the cloud is established by a salvo every 15 yards of front should receive 5 rounds per minute to ensure a continuous barrage. Experiment shows that this is best done by Battery Fire and not by firing Salvos.

    4.5" HOW. SHELL, FILLED W.P.

    With wind blowing on to objective one gun will cover 20 yards of front. A continuous barrage can be established and maintained over a given front by firing a salvo followed by Battery Fire, 10 secs., i.e., every 30 yards of front should receive 1 round per minute.

2.. Should the wind be blowing down the target -

    18-pdr. Battery will cover 150 yards of front.

    4.5" How. Battery will cover 800 yards of front.

    The same rate being employed as above.

****

Append. 12

SECRET.

52nd D.A. No. A/631.

Right Group.
Left Group.

1. 155th Brigade will recapture MOEUVRES this evening and consolidate line ridge E.20.b., Cemetery Support in E.14.d. AAA 157th Bde. will confer and consolidate Cemetery support as far as E.14.d.50.65 and capture railway line between HOBART and Cemetery support as far as E.14.d.50.65 and capture railway line between HOBART and Cemetery trenches.
Zero will be 1900 hours.
Artillery action will be as under -
   At Zero, 52nd Divisional Artillery will put down a barrage on LINE E.20.a.05.45 to E.14.a.30.65 till Zero plus 5 and will then creep forward 100 yards per 4 minutes till the line of the Canal from E.20.d.30.35 to E.15.c.15.60. is reached.
   4.5" Hows. will be 200 yrds. ahead of 18-prdrs.
   At zero plus 45, 9th and 181st Bdes will cease fire the remainder will form protective barrage E.14.a.20.65 - E.15.a.0.2. - then along Canal to E.20.d.8.5.

2. Zone tasks etc. will be as allotted by C.R.A. to Group Commanders.

3. Rates of fire - Zero to Zero plus 10 - INTENSE.
                   Zero plus 10 to Zero plus 45 NORMAL.
                   Zero plus 45 to Zero plus 105 - SLOW.
                   then as situation demands.

4. H.A. continue to bombard Canal from Zero to Zero plus 30, then form blocks at Lock4, in E.8.d., E.20.d.8.3. and HINDENBURG LINE E.16.d.10.85 to E.21.b.10.90. till Zero plus 105 and concentrations on HINDENBURG LINE and Canal at irregular intervals during the night.

5. Guards D.A. are forming a block barrage on lower half of E.26.b. West of Canal and 2nd G.D.A. are enfilading Canal in E.8.b. & d from Zero to Zero plus 105.

                                    [signature]
                                    Captain R.A.,
                            Brigade Major R.A., 52nd D.A.

19th Sept. 1918.

52nd Division 'G'
155th Inf. Bde.
Corps H.A.
Guards D.A.
2nd G.D.A.

(6392) Wt. W6192/P875 1,500,000 4/18 McA & W Ltd (E 2815) Forms W3091/4.   Army Form W.3091.

52 Div

Cover for Documents.

Nature of Enclosures.

56 Bde R.F.A
Oct 1918

Notes, or Letters written.

Confidential.

VOLUME IV
PART X

WAR DIARY

from 1st.October, 1918

to 31st.October, 1918.

56th.BRIGADE, R. F. A.

Battye
for a/Lieut.Colonel, R.F.A.
Commanding 56th.Brigade, R. F. A.

56th Bde RFA
Vol IV Part X

Army Form C. 2118.

WAR DIARY
INTELLIGENCE SUMMARY.
(Erase heading not required.)

Instructions regarding War Diaries and Intelligence Summaries are contained in F.S. Regs., Part II. and the Staff Manual respectively. Title pages will be prepared in manuscript.

Place	Date	Hour	Summary of Events and Information	Remarks and references to Appendices
CANTAING	1-10-18		Batteries advanced to positions as shewn on Map I & fired Barrage in accordance with Appendix I. 52nd Div Inf in line	Appendix I
	2-10-18		No 28668 Gr Toes W & No 125494 Dr Thompson G. 527 Battery RFA wounded. Brigade quipped with 9' Brigade RFA	IV Appendix II
	3-10-18		Batteries fired Barrage at 23 Hours in support of 155 Inf Brigade. see Appendix II. 527 Battery RFA 27 horses killed by 1 H.V. shell. "C" 56 Battery RFA Lt B.P.Crombie RFA joined & posted to "C" 56 Battery RFA	IV IV IV
	4-10-18		N.L	IV
" "	5-10 -18		Batteries ordered into rest & marched to vicinity of LONGUEVAL in vicinity of MOEUVRES	
	6-10-18		Batteries ordered out of rest & came into action near NOYELLES see Maps I & II in support of 63rd Division. Lt W.B. Collier DCM RFA joined & posted to C/56 RFA No1563621 Dr Hookins J 261756 Hughes D. Killed in action No 4735 Sgt Jackson W. G.S.W. slight all C/56 No 207210 Gr Stoneax G wounded B/56. 6 men of B/56 gassed.	IV.I
NOYELLES	7-10-18		Batteries rested in action	

Confidential

Army Form C. 2118.

56ᵗʰ Bde. R.F.A.
Vol III Part X

WAR DIARY
or
INTELLIGENCE SUMMARY.
(Erase heading not required.)

Instructions regarding War Diaries and Intelligence Summaries are contained in F. S. Regs., Part II. and the Staff Manual respectively. Title pages will be prepared in manuscript.

Place	Date	Hour	Summary of Events and Information	Remarks and references to Appendices
NOYELLES	8-10-18		Batteries fired Barrage 5am in support of 63ʳᵈ Division	J.J App VI
AWOINGT	9-10-18		Batteries advanced see Map II to AWOINGT & came into action in support of 73ʳᵈ Brigade of 24ᵗʰ Division	J.J App VI
AWOINGT	10-10-18	0500	Batteries fired Barrage in support of 73ʳᵈ Brigade advancing on CAGNONCLES advanced 1000 yds relid at LA BALOTTE into action near VAQUES BRIDGE advanced 1800 hours & came	J.J
VAQUES Bridge	11-10-18	0800	Fired on S.ᵗ AUBERT in support of 17ᵗʰ Infantry Brigade. Following casualties 8-10-18 No 267902 G.ʳ Palmer J 700910 G.ʳ Holden M.T TODDE all C/56ᵗʰ 12026 B.ʳ Coleman E B/56 wounded No 66471 Sgᵗ Turner J A/56 No 25994 J G.ʳ Wilson A/56 Both wounded 9-10-18 9-10-18 L/Lᵗ B Gell C/56 K illed in action No 891436 G.ʳ Rogers C/56 wounded No 89561 G.ʳ Hillyer C/56 wounded No 242187 G.ʳ Genn E C/56 wounded 10-10-18 No 39154 G.ʳ Blanchard A/56 wounded No 174513 G.ʳ Bixen J A/56 wounded No 77014 G.ʳ Stretch A/56 wounded No 2625 Sgᵗ Jenns W. D. B/56 wounded No 30510 G.ʳ Clarke A B/56 wounded No 125569 G.ʳ Thorpson T.K B/56 Killed No 74343 G.ʳ Perry J B/56 K illed No 1335¹ G.ʳ Vaughan H B/56 Killed No 62285 G.ʳ Waddle J 527 wounded No 133/5¹ G.ʳ Grundy A/527 wounded No 5185 B.ʳ Spurdd A 527 Killed	J.J

Army Form C. 2118.

Confidential

56th Brigade RFA
Vol XIV Part X

WAR DIARY
or
INTELLIGENCE SUMMARY.
(Erase heading not required.)

Instructions regarding War Diaries and Intelligence Summaries are contained in F.S. Regs., Part II. and the Staff Manual respectively. Title pages will be prepared in manuscript.

Place	Date	Hour	Summary of Events and Information	Remarks and references to Appendices
VACQUES BRIDGE	11-10/18		No 147137 G^r Alexander B 527 Killed No 104391 G^r Stackie A 527 Killed No 187963 G^r Evard Q P wounded A/56 No 119183 G^r Kelly T A/56 wounded No 26052 Lt B^r Scott GB/56 wounded No 223164 G^r Gargett P.T. B/56 wounded No 223269 G^r Burton E c/56 wounded No 90954 G^r Thorne T c/56 wounded No 01940 G^r Elsa T c/56 wounded	J.T.J
S^T AUBERT	12-10-18		Batteries advanced from Vacques Bridge 1200 & came into action East of S^T AUBERT in following positions see Map III At 1820 fired Bombardment as in Appendix III in support of 17th Infantry Brigade who later endeavoured to force crossings over L^A SELLE Following casualties Lt W.B. Collier c/56 wounded Capt C.H. Button 527 wounded No 2644 G^r Hire E 527 wounded No 62847 G^r Hanson W 527 wounded No 218552 G^r Robbins A.G wounded 527.	J.T.J Appendix III J.T.J
S^T AUBERT	13-10-18		Batteries in action as before fired barrage at 2.00 Hours 16 2025 Hours in support of 72nd Infantry Brigade who endeavoured to seize line of Railway on line V.H. a O.O.	J.T.J
S^T AUBERT	14-10-18		Batteries fired much harassing fire in support of 72nd Infantry Brigade endeavouring to filter into HAUSSY VILLAGE	
ST. AUBERT	15-10-18		Batteries fired in support of 17th Infantry Brigade who attempted to dribble into	

Army Form C. 2118.

56th Bde. RFA
Vol IV Part 10

WAR DIARY
or
INTELLIGENCE SUMMARY.
(Erase heading not required.)

Confidential

Instructions regarding War Diaries and Intelligence Summaries are contained in F. S. Regs., Part II. and the Staff Manual respectively. Title pages will be prepared in manuscript.

Place	Date	Hour	Summary of Events and Information	Remarks and references to Appendices
St AUBERT	15-10-18		Following casualties 7856 Gr Milne A/56 wounded 9/076 Sgt Daniels B/56 wounded 1999 Cpl James W c/56 wounded. One Section B/56 forward to V14 d.90.80.	Th.1
	16-10-18		Batteries fired Barrage 0520 hours in support of Royal West Kent regiment 24th division who attacked HAUSSY & gained their objective but had to withdraw after dark. Following casualties No 78941 105218 Gr Humphries B/56 wounded Gr 217602 No 214192 Gr Roth G c/56 wounded No 22890 Cpl Davenport Johnston R c/56 Killed No 633983 Gr P. Tendrigh A 527 wounded W.C. 527 wounded Gr 141363 Hawes R c/56 wounded	T.1
	17-10-18		Batteries relieved by 315 Army Brigade RFA & marched into rest at PROVILLE SOUTH of Cambrai. Lt Carrington Pierce promoted Captain. to remain in B/56	T.1
PROVILLE	18-10-18		Batteries rested	Appendix III
VAUX VRAUCOURT	19-10-18		Brigade marched to and camped at VAUX VRAUCOURT	Appendix IV
	20-10-18		Brigade entrained at FREMICOURT for ACQ	
LA TARGETTE	21-10-18		Brigade marched & went into old wagon lines at LA TARGETTE Cross Roads	
	22-10-18		Maj. General Alexander 1st Army visited Batteries	Batteries rested. Th.1
	23-10-18		Batteries rested 2/Lt Buckley A/56 posted to H.Q Portuguese Army	T.1

Army Form C. 2118.

56th Bde RFA
Vol IV Part 10

WAR DIARY
or
INTELLIGENCE SUMMARY.
(Erase heading not required.)

Place	Date	Hour	Summary of Events and Information	Remarks and references to Appendices
AUBY	24-10-18		Brigade marched & went into Billets at AUBY	JLI
	25-10-16		Brigade marched to Dorcy & went into Billets A/56 Bde R.F.A.	
FRAIS MARAIS	26-10-18		Brigade marched to and went into Billets at FRAIS MARAIS 3 miles North East of DOUAI. 11 reinforcements received.	JLJ
	27-10-18		Brigade visited by Brigadier General Coe 52nd Divn. Comdg Wks BGRA VIII Corps. 62 reinforcements received	JLJ
	28-10-18		Brigade visited 7 reinforcements posted to Brigade.	JLI T
	29-10-16		N.L.	
	30-10-18		Brigade & Battery Commanders inspected 63rd Brigade R.F.A. positions at Mont du Puy J.27.d. Sheet 44 doors. 4 R. reinforcements received	JLM
	31-10-16		N.L. 3 Reinforcements received	JLK

TL Gordon
Lt Col
Comdg 56th Bde
RFA

Appendix I October

SECRET.

63RD (R.N.) DIVISIONAL ARTY. OPERATION ORDER NO.3.
****

1st October 1918.

52nd Division will attack through the 63rd (R.N.) Division this afternoon.

ZERO HOUR will be 5.44 p.m.

The attack will be covered by a creeping barrage as under :-

At ZERO the barrage comes down on the line A.27.c.8.0. to A.21.c.8.0., and remains there till ZERO plus 36 minutes, during which time the Infantry will work up close to it.

At ZERO plus 36, it lifts forward due East 100 yards every four minutes to the line of the protective barrage A.28.c.20.00. - A.28.a.20.00. - A.22.c.50.00. *At Z+52 the barrage will rest for 4 mins. i.e lifting at +56 instead of +52*

4.5" Hows. come down 200 yards East of the 18 pdrs. and move forward with them, keeping 200 yds. ahead.

The 4.5" How.Battery of 72nd Brigade will move along the trench in A.27.b. and A.28. a & b.

On arrival on the line of protective barrage fire will search forward, slacken gradually, and cease.

From Zero to Zero plus 36 the 18 pdr.Batteries of 9th and 56th Brigades will search forward and back to the opening line in 50 yard lifts, and then move forward according to orders.

Lanes are as under :-

72nd { 9th }					
	26	27 A	28	29	30
315th { 56th }					

P.T.O.

2.

Rates :- Zero to Zero plus 36 :- Normal.
        Z plus 36 to Z plus 40 :- Intense.
        Z plus 40 to Z plus 52 :- Rapid.
        Z plus 52 to Z plus 68 :- Normal.

Ammunition :- 50% "A", 50% "AX".
        Smoke will be fired throughout the barrage, if available in time.
(There is none at the A.R.P. at present).

R.G.A. programme is being arranged by Corps.

Artillery Brigades to acknowledge.

                                            Major R.A.,
                                          Brigade Major,
                           63rd (R.N.) Divisional Artillery.

SECRET.   COPY NO...

52ND DIVISIONAL ARTILLERY ORDER NO. 40.

1. 155th Infantry Brigade will attack and capture FOUBOURG DE PARIS this evening.
   The attack will take place from the south-west, the forming up line being A.27.a.4.2. to A.27.c.9.0.
   The objective is the FOUBOURG DE PARIS, as far north as line A.21.d.0.0. - A.22.c.2.6.

2. The attack will be supported by a switching bombardment of Heavy Artillery and 4.5" Howitzers and covered by a protective barrage of 18-pdrs.
   Tasks for this are shown in bombardment table attached.
   57th D.A. are co-operating by firing on trenches in northern half A.21.c. and on trench A.15.d.0.0. to A.21.b.9.6. from Zero plus 10 to Zero plus 100.

3. Zero hour will be 2300.

4. Watches will be synchronised from this office.

5. S.O.S. lines after attack will be :-

   18-pdrs - A.21.b.6.2. - A.22.c.5.9. - A.28.c.4.0. - A.27.d.5.0.
   4.5" Hows. - 200 yards outside 18-pdr line.
   9th Brigade Group will be super-imposed on 72nd Brigade Group.
   Heavy Artillery - road A.28.c. A.28.a. A.28.b. A.22.d.

6. ACKNOWLEDGE.

                                    (signed)
                                    Captain R.A.
                                    Brigade Major R.A., 52nd Divn:

3rd October 1918.
Issued 2.10 pm.
DISTRIBUTION.
  Copies No. 1/10 9th Bde RFA.
            11/20 72nd Bde RFA.
               21 52nd Division 'G'.
               22 32nd Bde RGA.
               23 XVII Corps R.A.
               24 XVII Corps H.A.
               25 2nd D.A.
               26 57th D.A.
               27 155th Inf. Bde.
            28/29 War Diary.
               30 File.

TIME.	HEAVY ARTY. TASKS.	8th BRIGADE GROUP TASKS. 4.5 Hows.	18-pdrs.	7th BRIGADE GROUP TASKS. 4.5 Hows.	18-pdrs.	RATE OF FIRE.
Zero to plus 10	A.27.b.30.40 — A.27.b.40.20 — 55.70. A.27.b.50.45.		A.27.b.40.20 — A.27.b.50.45.			
Plus 10 to plus 25.	A.27.b.3.8 — A.21.d.7.0 — A.27.b.55.70 — A.27.b.80.85.	Hedgerows A.27.d.25.35 — A.23.c.20.40 & A.27.d.7.8 tp A.28.c.4.4.	A.27.b.55.70 — A.27.b.80.85.	A.28.a.1.6 — A.28.c.5.9. A.28.a.0.4. A.28.c.9.3.	4.5" Howitzers.	
Plus 25 to plus 40.	Factory and road A.21.d.7.3 — A.21.d.8.4.	A.21.d.7.0 to A.21.d.8.2.		A.21.d.7.0 to A.21.d.8.2.	—do—	'b' to plus 75 —Normal. plus 75 to plus 110 — Slow.
Plus 40 to plus 75.	A.22.c.1.3 — A.22.c.1.1.	A.21.d.8.4 — A.21.d.95.70.	—do—	A.21.d.8.4 — A.21.d.95.70.	.fire to move Normal with 4.5 Hows.after plus 35.	18-pdrs.
Plus 75 to plus 110.		A.22.c.1.9 — A.22.c.1.1.	—do—	A.22.c.1.9 — A.22.c.1.1.	—do—	9th Bde Group. plus 10 to plus 25 — NORMAL. plus 25 to plus 90 — SLOW. plus 90 to plus 110 — VERY SLOW.
				guns on northern half. plus 10 to plus 90 —SLOW. plus 90 to plus 110— VERY SLOW.		72nd Bde Group. guns on southern half. plus 10 to plus 35 — NORMAL. plus 35 to plus 90 — SLOW. plus 90 to plus 110— VERY SLOW.

1. The Brigade will march to MORCHIES area on 19th inst.

2. Starting point on road outside C Battery camp

3. Order of march and time of reaching starting point

   Headquarters.   1038 ~~1010~~ hrs
       A   ~~1030~~
       B   1035
       C   1040
       J-27.   1045

4. Route:
   Canal crossing Complete 3.
   ~~Canal crossing F 30 a 5 5 - CANTAING - outskirts FONTAINE NOTR. - the~~

5. Halts.
   ~~1st halt 1130 and~~ at hours interval
   Starting 1130.. Time of halt for feeding will be notified ~~on the march~~

6. Complete 5-

7. " 8.

8. An officer of each Battery with Collecting Party, will report ready ~~at starting~~ point at ~~10.30~~ 10.25

9. 9 complete

10. ack

SECRET.   62nd D.A. A/275.

8th Brigade RFA.
330th Brigade RFA.
~~315th Brigade R.F.A.~~
72nd Brigade RFA.

Please make all preparations for firing attached barrage.
Should the infantry forming up line be altered, the barrage will
be opened 250 yards ahead of it and move in initial lifts of 100 yards
till it meets opening line shown on tracing and then conforms to tracing.

Lifts will be 100 yards every 3 minutes until the 30 minute halt
is reached and then 100 yards every 4 minutes when it starts moving
forward again.

4.5" Howitzers will be 200 yards in front of 18-pdr. barrage
and conform to it.

18-pdrs will fire shrapnel and smoke only.

The above are all the details available at present.

72nd and ~~315th Brigades~~ will probably start advancing when their
range reaches 7,000 yards.

                                          W.G. Harrison
                                          Captain D.A.
                                          Brigade Major R.A., 62nd Divn.
8th October 1918.

    Notification has been received from Corps that this
barrage will be altered and that 315 Bde will not take part.
    The general trend is very much the same.

SECRET. 52nd R.A. No. S.G.2922.

9th Bde. R.F.A.
56th Bde. R.F.A.
72nd A.F.A.Bde. (A)
315th A.F.A.Bde. (C)
52nd D.A.C.
9th Bde. Wagon Lines.

AMMUNITION.

Batteries will complete dumps at guns forthwith to the following amounts:-

    30 AS.)
    320 A.)   per gun.
    200 BX.   per howitzer.

Echelons will be kept full with 80% A and 80% AX except that 52nd D.A.C. will carry 400 AS and 160 BOG instead of some of the A, AX and BX.

72nd and 315th Brigades already have sufficient AS to carry out the above.

9th Brigade Wagon Lines are collecting tomorrow, 6th instant, the 401 rounds AS left in 9th Bde. positions tonight and will send up to guns on night of 6th instant.

In addition 9th Bde. Wagon Line are salving 206 AS from 56th Bde. old positions to send up to guns.

56th Brigade have 220 AS in their Echelons and D.A.C. will deliver 300 rounds (100 per battery) to 56th Bde. positions tomorrow night, 6th instant.

Smoke in/ possession must be equally distributed to batteries.

A small amount of AS is expected at A.R.P., F.20.a., tomorrow.

D.A.C. Section Commanders will be at this Headquarters at 10.0 AM tomorrow and will be shown the new positions for 56th Bde. R.F.A. into which the D.A.C. will dump 200 rounds A per gun or as near that as possible tomorrow night, 6th instant, after dusk.

5th October, 1918.
                              Captain R.A.
                      Staff Captain R.A., 52nd Division.

56 Bde *Tracing Y to follow.*
Tracing X is barrage map as issued.

S E C R E T.

63RD (R.N.) DIVISIONAL ARTILLERY INSTRUCTIONS No.1.
****

6th October 1918.

1. INFORMATION.

The Third Army will continue the attack at a date and time which will be notified.

2. INTENTION.

63rd (R.N.) Division will attack and capture NIERGNIES and establish themselves on the CAMBRAI-FORENVILLE Road to the East of it.

Details of objectives and boundaries are shown on tracing "X" attached.

188th Inf.Bde. will be on the right, 189th Inf.Bde. on the left, 190th Inf.Bde. in support.

63rd Battalion M.G.C. are providing an overhead barrage.

3. ARTILLERY.

The Artillery co-operating is as follows :-

(a) FIELD ARTILLERY.
Right (52nd D.A.)Group.... H.Q. F.27.c.00.35.
Left (57th D.A.)Group.... H.Q. F.15.c.00.00.

(b) HEAVY ARTILLERY, affiliated to 63rd (R.N.) Division -
35th Brigade R.G.A.
Corps Group. 62nd, 66th, and COTTER's Brigades R.G.A.

Tasks for the Artillery Groups are as shewn on tracing "X" and Table "A" attached.

A creeping barrage will be put down by the 18 pdrs. and 4.5" howitzers, formed by :-
Right Group.... 9th, 56th and 72nd Brigades R.F.A.
Left Group..... 74th, 181st and 2nd N.Z.Brigades R.F.A.
178th Bde.R.F.A. will form a special smoke screen on the left flank.

93rd Bde. and D/315th Bty. R.F.A. will engage all known and likely M.G.emplacements on the left flank of the attack.(See tracing "Y")

The 315th Army Bde.R.F.A., less D/315, will be under the 57th Division from Zero to Zero plus 60 mins., at which time it will come under the orders of C.R.A., 63rd (R.N.) Division and fire on tasks as shewn in tracing "Y".

The initial 18 pdr.barrage will come down at ZERO, 300 yards over the Infantry jumping off line. It will rest there for 10 minutes, then creep forward at the rate of 100 yards in four minutes to a protective line covering the first objective (RED).

It will rest on this line for 30 minutes, when it will move and swing forward again as shown in tracing "X" attached, to the final protective barrage line, when batteries will lift on to targets which will be allotted to them.

1. 3. contd..........

2.

4.5" Howrs. will conform to the pace of the 18 pdr. barrage, and will come down on points (see tracing "Y") at a distance of not less than 200 yards East of it.

4. LIAISON.
The 72nd Bde.R.F.A. will be in liaison with the 188th (Right)Inf.Bde., and the 178th Bde.R.F.A. with the left (189th) Inf.Bde.
Brigade Commanders will be with G.O's.C. Infantry Brigades on "Y-Z" night. Locations will be issued when selected.

5. ADVANCE.
One Battery from the 72nd and 178th Brigades R.F.A. will advance at ZERO plus 30 minutes, to act as batteries in close support of the Infantry. The remainder of those Brigades will advance to the Valley in G.4. and G.10. when the first objective is gained.

6. TANKS.
Seven tanks follow the Infantry to the first objective (RED) and precede them to the second objective (GREEN).

7. Advanced Division and Divisional Artillery H.Q. will be at L.10.d.9.3.

8. Artillery to acknowledge.

J. C. Walford
Major R.A.,
Brigade Major,
63rd (R.N.) Divisional Artillery.

Copies to -
    R.A., XVII Corps,
    63rd (R.N.) Division.
    XVII C.H.A.
    57th D.A.,
    2nd D.A.,
    9th Bde.R.F.A.)
    56th "   ") Right Group.X
    72nd "   ")
    74th Bde.R.F.A.)
    181st "   ") Left Group.
    2nd N.Z. "   )
    315th Army Bde.R.F.A.X
    178th Bde.R.F.A.,
    93rd Bde.R.F.A.
    35th Bde.R.G.A.
    188th Inf.Bde.
    189th "   "
    190th "   "
    63rd M.G.Bn.
    O.i/c.Sigs., 63rd D.A.
    War Diary.
    File.

S E C R E T.   TABLE "A". CREEPING BARRAGE.
(To accompany 63rd (R.N.) Div.Arty.Instructions No.1.)

UNIT.	TIME.	TASK.	RATE.	PACE.	ALGN.	REMARKS.
RIGHT GROUP. 9th,56th,72nd Brigades.	Z to Z plus 10 mins.	Bombard the line G.17.b.00.55.— G.10.b.70.00.	INTENSE. Z + 5 to Z + 10. RAPID.	—	"A".	6% smoke.
	Z + 10 to Z + 74.	Creep forward along lane.	Slow in the open, rapid on trenches or villages.	100 yards in four mins.	"	
	Z + 86 to Z + 118.	Bombard on first protective barrage.(DOTTED RED).	INTENSE first 5 mins. then RAPID.	—	"	As the fire of each Bde reaches the dotted BLUE line it will reform on to its own portion of the final protective barrage.
	Z + 116 to arrival on final protective.	Creep & swing on to final protective barrage. (DOTTED BLUE)	SLOW in open, RAPID on trenches & villages.	100 yds. in 4 mins.	"	
LEFT GROUP. 2nd N.Z.Bde. 74th " 181st "	Z to Z plus 10.	Bombard the line G.10.b.70.00.— G.4.c.25.60.	AS FOR RIGHT GROUP.			

CONTINUES AS FOR RIGHT GROUP.

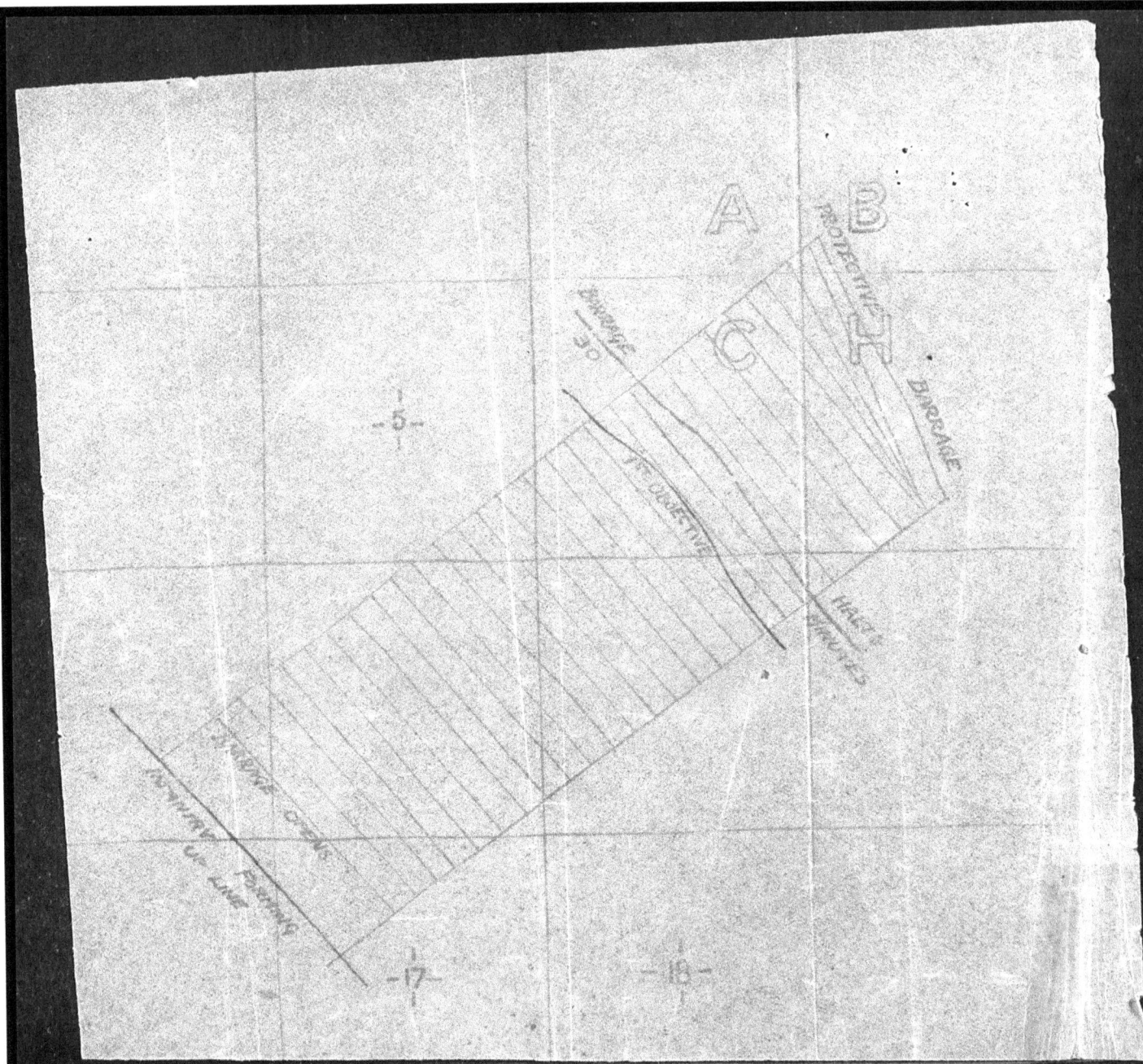

"A" Form
MESSAGES AND SIGNALS.

Army Form C. 2121 (in pads of 100.)

TO
52 DAC
56 M Bde

Sender's Number: SC 247
Day of Month: 6

40th DA will draw 200 AS from you today leaving only 200 AS to deliver to 56th Bde tonight. You will deliver full echelon B+ to 56th Bde i.e. 1088 rounds added DAC reply 56 Bde

From / Place: 52 DA

S E C R E T.

ADDENDA TO TABLE "A"
accompanying
63RD (R.N.) DIVISIONAL ARTY. INSTRUCTIONS No.1.

6th Oct.1918.

95th Brigade and D/315th Battery, see tracing "Y".
315th Brigade R.F.A. less D/315 are under C.R.A., 57th Division until ZERO plus 60 minutes.

178th Brigade smoke screen will be put down 200 yards clear of the left flank of the 63rd Division, and will be continued until each Battery moves forward as detailed in para.5.

In all cases fire will search forward to limits of range and gradually cease on arrival at final protective barrage line.

J.C. Walford
Major R.A.,
Brigade Major,
63rd (R.N.) Divisional Artillery.

Copies to All Recipients of 63rd (R.N.) D.A.
Instructions No.1.

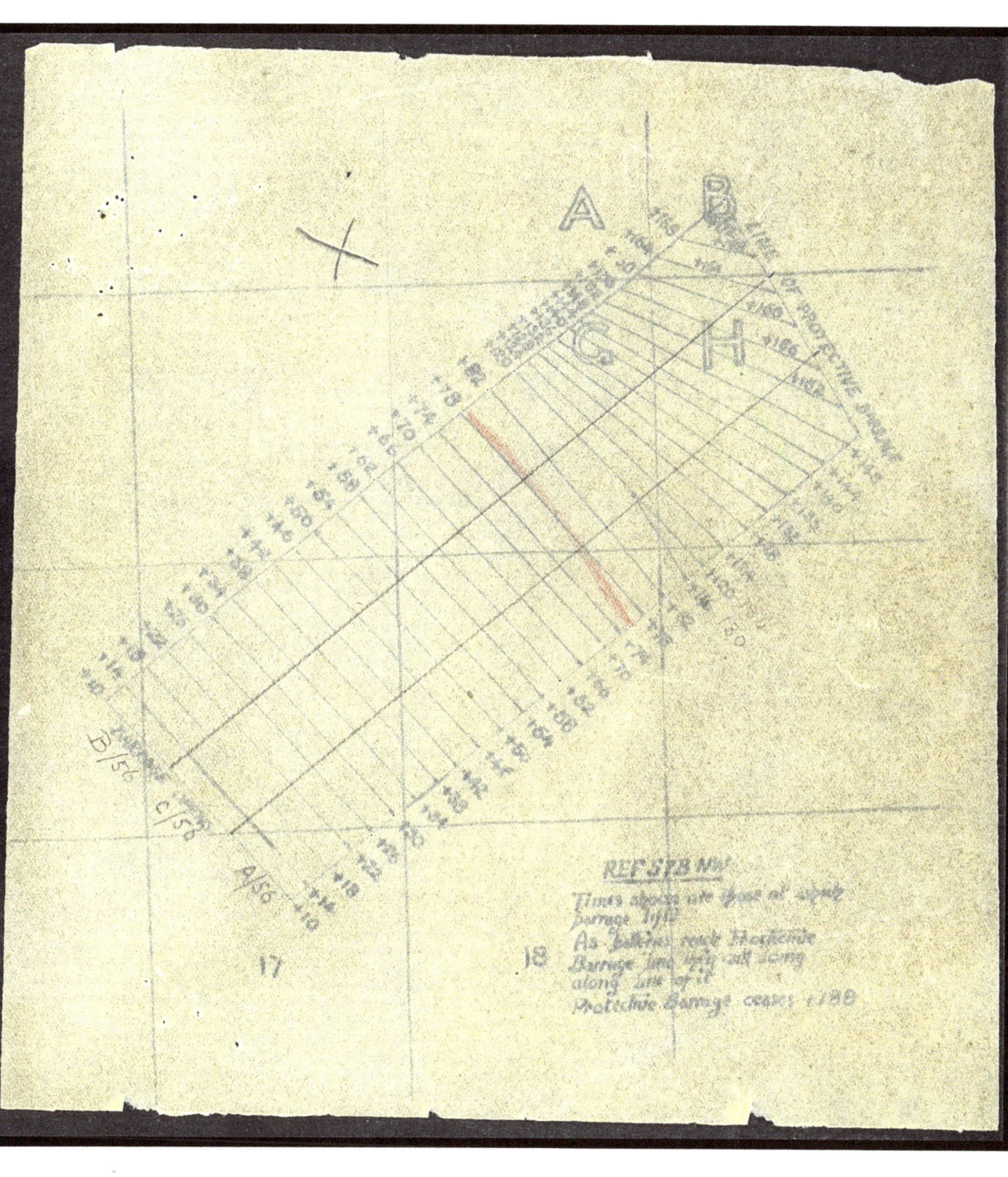

S E C R E T.

AMENDMENT No.2. TO
63RD (R.N.) DIVISIONAL ARTY. INSTRUCTIONS No.1.

7th October 1918.

On the left Artillery Group front, the 18 pdr. barrage will now come down along the following line, and not as originally issued in tracing "X":-

G.10.b.70.05. - G.10.a.10.90. - G.3.a.9.3.

It will remain on this line from Zero to Zero plus 3 mins., then lifting to the line :-

G.10.b.70.05. - G.4.c.30.20. - G.4.c.10.50., from Zero plus 3 to Zero plus 6 mins.

At Zero plus 6 mins. it lifts to the BLUE line (original Zero line) remaining on till Zero plus 10 and then moving forward as already ordered.

Artillery to acknowledge.

J. C. Walford
Major R.A.,
Brigade Major,
63rd (R.N.) Divisional Artillery.

Copies to All Recipients of 63rd (R.N.) Divisional
Artillery Instructions No.1.

Divisional Artillery H.Q. will open at L.10.d.1.3.
at 5.0 p.m.

56.-

S E C R E T.

AMENDMENT No.3 TO
63RD (R.N.) DIVISIONAL ARTY. INSTRUCTIONS No.1.

7th October 1918.

Reference Artillery Instructions No.1 and tracing "X".

The length of the pause covering the first objective (DOTTED RED Line) will now be 44 minutes and NOT 50 minutes.

Artillery to acknowledge.

J. C. Walford
Major R.A.,
Brigade Major,
63rd (R.N.) Divisional Artillery.

Copies to all recipients of 63rd (R.N.) Div.Arty. Instructions No.1.

56th Bay

S E C R E T.

63RD (R.N.) DIVISIONAL ARTY.INSTRUCTIONS No.2.
****

6th Oct.1918.

1. With reference to para.4 of 63rd D.A.Instructions No.1, H.Q. of all Infantry Brigades will be at Mt.sur l'OEUVRE.(G.8.b.)

2. A central visual station will be established in G.2.b. to work between D.A.Groups and to 63rd D.A.H.Q.

3. 72nd Bde.R.F.A. crossing the CANAL will use the bridges at NOYELLES in L.11.d.8.2. and L.12.c.7.2.; 178th Bde. those in L.6.c.1.4. and L.6.c.3.2. Approaches must be reconnoitred.
   Mobile trench mortars will report to H.Q., Right (188th) Inf.Bde.

4. O's.c. Artillery Brigades in liaison with Infantry Brigades will detail sections for each battalion of the attacking Brigades, and must issue instructions for close co-operation with Battalion Commanders. Opportunities for the employment of these sections are most likely to occur when the barrage programme is completed, and O.P's from which the situation can be seen should be selected at the earliest moment to obtain useful results.

5. Attention is particularly drawn to XVII Corps R.A.No.23/5 of 2nd Oct. on one subject of reporting and collecting from *information* Artillery sources with punctuality.

J. C. Walford
Major R.A.,
Bde.Major,
63rd (R.N.) Divisional Arty.

Copies to -
R.A., XVII Corps.
63rd (R.N.) Divn., 188, 189th, 190th Inf.Bdes.
52nd D.A.Group.
57th D.A.Group.
35th Bde.R.G.A.

all Battys

No 04/88

Herewith Barrage tracing. The 18pr zone has been divided equally into 3 tasks.
Copies of 63rd R.N. D Inst No 1 & 2 are forwarded for information.
Battys should reconnoitre to day forward wagon lines positions in vicinity of N.W.E. 6.000

& which leavest men coms to up advised in april
of an advance
As J-27 How Batty cannot reach their final
task they will form a protective barrage.
200 x East of final 18 pr protective barrage
ack.

[signature]

7.10.18
1300hrs

56 Boe

S E C R E T.

AMENDMENT No.1. TO
63RD (R.N.) DIVISIONAL ARTY. INSTRUCTIONS No.2.
****

7th October 1918.

Cancel first three lines of para.3, and substitute the following :-

"The 72nd Army Bde.R.F.A. will cross the Canal by the bridge at F.29.b.7.5. ; 178th Bde.R.F.A. by that at F.23.d.99.70. and the 74th Bde.R.F.A. (when ordered) by the bridge at L.6.c.1.4.
Approaches must be reconnoitred."

Major R.A.,
Brigade Major,
63rd (R.N.) Divisional Artillery.

Copies to All Recipients of 63rd (R.N.) Divisional
Artillery Instructions No.2.

SECRET.   52nd D.A. No. A/277.

9th Brigade RFA (5)
86th Brigade RFA (5)
72nd Army Brigade RFA.(5)

Herewith barrage tracing.
4.5" Howitzers will fire on selected points which will be notified later and keep 200 yards ahead of 18-pdrs and should consequently be given a copy of this.

Rates of fire will be :-

Zero to Zero plus 5 - INTENSE.

Plus 5 to plus 30 - RAPID.

Plus 30 to plus 70 - SLOW.

Plus 70 to plus 90 - RAPID.

Plus 90 to plus 120 - SLOW.

Plus 120 to plus 148 RAPID.

Plus 148 to plus 188 SLOW.

18-pdrs fire 6% smoke, remainder shrapnel.

Brigades will be superimposed upon each other across whole front.

ACKNOWLEDGE by wire.

                                                Captain R.A.
                                        Brigade Major R.A., 52nd Divn:

8th October 1918.

52nd D.A. No. Z/676.

9th Brigade RFA.
56th Brigade RFA.
72nd Army Brigade RFA.
315th Army Brigade RFA.   52nd D.A.C.
===============================   ==========

The following bridges in NOYELLES area are reported fit for Field Guns. -

    Over river - L.5.d.3.7.
               L.11.b.65.70.
               L.11.d.80.15.

    Over canal - L.6.c.1.3.   Pontoon.
               L.6.c.30.25.   Pontoon.
               L.5.b.8.1.
               L.12.c.65.20.

The best crossing in this area is at L.11.d.80.15 and L.12.c.65.20.

                                             Captain R.A.
                                             Brigade Major R.A.
                                             52nd Division.

6th October 1918.

"A" Form
MESSAGES AND SIGNALS.

Army Form C. 2121 (in pads of 100.)

Arrange to include

~~New line trench G 5d 83~~
~~to G 12a 5.7 aaa~~
~~M 45 G 11 b 38 23 aaa~~

4 to 6 anti tank guns oz
lie G 12b 55 G 6 a 5.5 d.o.o.

SECRET.

LOCATIONS OF 52ND DIVISIONAL ARTILLERY.
7/10/18.

	Location.	Wagon Lines	O.Ps.
H.Q., 52nd Div'l Arty.	F.27.c.00.25.	-	-
9th Bde., R.F.A. H.Q.	F.30.c.60.20	L.1.a.9.5.	A.26.d.60.00.
19th Battery R.F.A.	L.6.a.50.50.	L.1.d.80.50.	-
20th Battery R.F.A.	F.30.a.91.05.	K.12.d.	-
28th Battery R.F.A.	L.6.c.89.97.	L.1.b.	-
D/69th Battery.RFA.	L.6.a.80.71.	L.1.a.	-
56th Bde R.F.A. H.Q.	L.11.d.80.80.	L.1.d.	A.26.d.70.00.
"A" Battery R.F.A.	G.7.c.00.50.	L.1.d.	-
"B" Battery R.F.A.	L.12.c.15.80.	L.1.d.	-
"C" Battery R.F.A.	G.7.b.30.20.	L.1.b.	-
527th Battery R.F.A.	L.12.c.65.75.	L.2.b.	-
72nd Army Bde R.F.A. H.Q.	F.20.a.9.5.		(A.26.d.9.1.
A/72nd Battery R.F.A.	F.28.d.7.7.	E.30.a.	(A.26.a.6.4.
B/72nd Battery R.F.A.	L.4.b.2.5.	E.30.b.	-
C/72nd Battery R.F.A.	L.4.b.50.95.	E.30.c.	-
D/72nd Battery R.F.A.	F.29.c.2.6.		-
B.A.C.	-	F.20.c.4.5.	-
315th Bde R.F.A. H.Q.	F.28.c.2.4.	F.20.c.7.3.	A.19.d.90.05.
A/315 Battery R.F.A.	F.28.b.10.75.	F.25.d.5.5.	-
B/315 Battery R.F.A.	F.28.d.7.5.	F.25.c.8.3.	-
C/315 Battery R.F.A.	F.28.a.70.90.	F.21.a.05.50.	A.26.c.50.75.
D/315 Battery R.F.A.	A.22.d.7.7.	K.6.b.9.5.	A.20.c.0.1.
B.A.C.	-	F.20.c.4.5.	-
52nd D.T.M.O.	E.21.d.40.25.	-	-
52nd D.A.C. H.Q.	E.21.d.8.0.	-	-
No.1 Section.	E.21.d.8.2.	-	-
No.2.Section.	E.21.d.4.2.	-	-
S.A.A.Section.	L.2.a.0.3.	-	-

7/10/18.

H. Stanley.
2/Lieut, R.F.A.
Orderly Officer 9th Brigade R.F.A.

Copied and ~~adjusted~~ amended by 9th Bde R.F.A. Group.

Forwarded for information please

H Stanley 2/Lt R.F.A.
O O 9th Bde R.F.A.

"A" Form.
MESSAGES AND SIGNALS.

Army Form C. 2121.
(In pads of 100.)

TO: 171st Bde
      172 Bde
      3rd Bde

Sender's Number: F178   Day of Month: 7   AAA

Reference 63 DA. instrns:
aaa Tracing &
& allotment now Tasks
herewith aaa acknowledge

From Place: 52 DA

TO ALL RECIPIENTS OF 63RD (R.N.) DIV.ARTY.
INSTRUCTIONS No.1.
****

ZERO HOUR will be 04.30 hrs on 8th October 1918.

Artillery to acknowledge by wire.

J.C. Wargrave
Major R.A.,
Brigade Major,
63rd (R.N.) Divisional Artillery.

7th Oct.1918.

Amendment No 3.
AONO41
7183

12. Teams should not be unhooked until the train is in the Station and the exact position of the "flats" is known.
Each train contains 17 "flats" capable of holding about 59 pairs of wheels.

13. The Mortars and all personnel etc of D.T.M.C. will be entrained at VELU.

14. ACKNOWLEDGE.

                                                Captain R.A.,
19th October 1918.   Staff Captain R.A., 52nd Division.

DISTRIBUTION :-

        Copy No. 1 - 9th Bde RFA.
               2 - 56th Bde RFA.
               3 - D.A.C.
               4 - R.A.Sigs.
               5 - R.O.R.A.
               6 - 217 Coy A.S.C.
               7 - D.T.M.C.
               8 - Officer i/c entraining at VELU.
               9 -   "   "   "   "   FREMICOURT.
          10/11- War Diary.
              12 - File.

issued later

10 Acknowledge

Witnessed to Captain R.A.
Brigade Major R.A.
52nd Division

18.10.18

Distribution

9th Bde.
56th Bde
D. A?
D.T.M.O
217 Coy. A.S.C.
R.O. Sigs
R.O. R.A.
M. Diary
File

52nd Divisional Artillery Order No. 44

Reference sheet 57° N.E. map 1/40,000 hrs.

1. 52nd Div Arty will march to the MORCHIES area on 19th inst.

2. Order of march will be:-
   - 217 Coy. A.S.C.   starting 0900 hours.
   - 52 D.A.C.   starting 1000   "
   - 56 Bde. R.F.A.   starting 1030   "   Starting P
   - 9 Bde R.F.A.   starting 1100   "

   Starting point for each unit will be a point in present area to be selected by unit concerned.

3. Route will be:-
   Canal Crossing F.30.a.5.5.- CANTAING - outskirts FONTAINE-NOTRE-DAME, thence along CAMBRAI-BAPAUME road.

4. Brigades, 52nd D.A.C. & 217 Coy A.S.C. will march independently, unit commanders arranging their own halts etc.

5. 50 yds between sections will be maintained & every precaution against Hacking roads taken. March discipline will be carefully supervised.

6. Advance parties will report to S.C.R.A. HQ at 19h at the junction of the CAMBRAI-BAPAUME & the MORCHIES-BEAUMETZ roads.

7. D.T.M.O. and all Trench Mortar Personnel will march with and under orders of 52nd D.T.C. till further notice.

8. Rations for the 19th will be carried on men and animals.
   Rations for the 20th will be carried on train wagons under arrangements O.C. 217 Coy A.S.C. & delivered to units in new area on the evening 19th inst.

9. Entraining programme for 20th will be

Copy No. ___

17th Infantry Brigade Order No.253.

1. The 24th Division will continue the advance tomorrow 11th instant on LA SELLE River and establish bridgeheads on east bank. When completed the advance will be continued.

2. VI Corps will advance on a similar line and Canadian Corps has been directed on VALENCIENNES keeping touch with 24th Division just S. of CAMBRAI-SMULZON road and with left flank on Canal de L'ESCAUT.

3. 17th Brigade Group as under will form the advance guard :-

      17th Infantry Brigade.
      1 Brigade R.F.A.
      1 Section 60 pounders.
      1 Section 104th Field Coy. RE.
      'B' & 'C' Coys. 24th Bn. M.G.C.
      XVII Corps Cyclist Battalion
      1 Troop cavalry.

4. The Brigade Group will pass through troops of 73rd Brigade on the general line U.30.c. - U.16 as arranged with C.Os at the conference and will continue the advance by bounds as under :-

1st BOUND.
Road junction V.20.c. - ridge through V.13.b. - V.8.c and V.1.d. and b.

2nd BOUND.
Spur through V.15.d. - V.9.b. and V.3.a.

3rd BOUND.
Crossings of LA SELLE river and bridgeheads east of it.

4th BOUND.
High ground W.1.d. and spur running from it through W.1.b. and V.36.

5. 3rd Rifle Brigade will advance on the right, 1st Royal Fusiliers on the left. 8th Queens will be in reserve moving behind the left flank and paying particular attention to maintaining touch with the Brigade on our left.
    1 section R.F.A. and 1 section 17th L.T.M.Battery will accompany each leading battalion. 'C' Company 24th Battalion M.G.C. will accompany the right battalion under orders of C.O.3rd Bn. The Rifle Brigade.
    Sections R.F.A. will be at U.27.c.0.4 and U.19.d.8.6 respectively at 05.30 hours.

6. The Northern boundary of the Brigade is the CAMBRAI-SMULZOIR Road exclusive -
    The Southern boundary - HAUSSY inclusive - Cross roads MAISON BLANCHE W.1.d. inclusive - ESCARMAINE exclusive.

7. Inter-battalion boundary will be L'ERCLIN River - U.18.b.4.5. - Road fork V.7.d.8.4 - road through V.8.central (inclusive to 1st Royal Fus.) also wood in V.3.c. and V.9.a. (inclusive to 1st Royal Fus) - river crossing P.34.c.1.1 (inclusive to 1st Royal Fus)

8. XVII Corps Cyclist battalion will push forward at 05.00 hours on 11th inst. and will establish posts on the E. side of ST. AUBERT.

9. 'B' Coy. 24th Bn. M.G.C. will be at B.6.c.9.4 on the road at 05.00 hours on 11th inst.

10. 6th Dragoon Guards, in case of slight opposition being encountered are pushing forward to line of LA SELLE River to establish bridgeheads on the E. bank. They will also detail Officer patrols to maintain touch with the Divisions on our flanks.

11. 73rd Infantry Brigade with 1 Coy. 24th Bn. M.G.C. are also passing through the 73rd Infantry Brigade to follow 17th Infantry Brigade in close support.

-- 1 --

12.   Brigade and Battalion H.Q. will be established as under at 05.00 hours :-

          Brigade H.Q..............U.27.central.
          1st Bn. Royal Fusiliers........U.15.d.central.
          3rd Rifle Brigade   )
          'C' Coy. M.G.C.   ).............U.26.b.central.
          8th Queens...................U.20.d.60.90.

13.   Cable head will be established at 05.00 hours at Brigade H.Q. U.27.central. Cable will be extended along the AVESNES-ST.AUBERT-MONTRECOURT Roads.

14.   Information obtained from prisoners indicates that there are few of the enemy in front of us.
        The pursuit will be pressed on with the utmost vigour.

15.   ACKNOWLEDGE.

Issued to Sigs.   Captain,
at 1.45 hours.
12th October. 18.   Brigade Major, 17th Inf: Bde.

Copy No.1 to 8th Queens.   Copy No.2 to 1st Royal Fusiliers.
         3   3rd Rifle Bde.   4   17th L.T.M.Battery.
         5   Sigs. 17th I.B.   6   24th Divn. 'G' (2)
         7   103rd Field Coy.   8   74th Field Ambce.
         9   Att: Artillery Gp (2)   10   72nd Inf: Bde.
        11   73rd Inf: Bde.   12   6th Dragoon Gds.
        13   XVII Corps Cyclist Bn.   14   24th Bn. M.G.C.
        15   'D' Coy. M.G.C.   16   'C' Coy. M.G.C.
        17   Major Lagdon (2)   18   Major Hobdon (2)
        19   Brigade Major.   20   Staff Captain.
        21   I.O., 17th Inf: Bde.   22   War Diary.
        23   File.   24   Spare.
        25   Spare.   26   Spare.

56th. Brigade, RFA   M/178

All 56th. Bde. Batteries.
========================

1. The Brigade will march to MORCHIES area on 19th. instant.
2. Starting point on road outside C Battery's Camp.
3. Order of march, and time of reaching starting point

   Headquarters............1030 Hrs.
   A Battery...............1030 Hrs.
   B Battery...............1035 Hrs.
   C Battery...............1040 Hrs.
   527 How. Battery........1045 Hrs.

4. Route. Canal crossing F.30.a.5.5. - CANTAING - outskirts FONTAINE -NOTRE -DAME, thence along CAMBRAI-BAPAUME Road.
5. Halts. At hours interval starting 1130 hrs. Time of Halt for feeding will be notified on the march.
6. 40 yards between Sections will be maintained and every precaution against blocking roads taken.
   March discipline will be carefully supervised.
7. An officer of each Battery, with billeting party, will report to Adjutant at starting point at 1025 hrs.
8. Rations for the 19th. instant will be carried on men and animals.
   Rations for the 20th. will be carried on train wagons under arrangements O.C. 217 Coy. A.S.C. and delivered to units in new area on the evening of 19th. instant.
9. Entraining programme for 20th. will be issued later.
10. ACKNOWLEDGE.

Captain, RFA
Adjutant, 56th. Brigade, RFA

18th. October, 1918.

SECRET.   Copy No. 16 App VI

52ND DIVISIONAL ARTILLERY ORDER NO. 41.

1. At a date and zero hour to be notified later, the XVII Corps will attack in conjunction with the operations of Corps to south.

2. The 63rd R.N. Division will attack on a front of 1700 yards in a N.E. direction from a line G.4.c.0.1. to G.17.a.35.55.
   The first objective will be the trench running through G.8.a., c., 8.d. and G.12.b.
   The second objective is the road from H.1.d.0.4. to B.25.c.05.80 and the WOOD in A.30.c.
   The 57th Division will co-operate on the Left, their objective being the trench from G.4.a.0.8 to G.4.b.8.6.
   The 2nd Division will co-operate on the right, their objective being the same road as the 63rd Division, extending S.E. and including the village of FORENVILLE.

3. The 52nd D.A. Group consists of :-
      9th Brigade Group   ....   9th and 56th Brigades.
      72nd Brigade Group   ....   72nd and 315th Brigades.
   This Group will form the Right Group supporting the Right Brigade of 63rd Division (188th Inf. Bde.)
   315th Brigade RFA (less D/315) supports 57th Division till zero plus 60.
   The tasks and barrages for the above brigades are as shown on barrage tracings already issued.

4. 72nd Brigade RFA will be in liaison with 188th Inf. Bde.
   O.C., 72nd Brigade will report to G.O.C., 188th Inf. Bde on YZ night at MONT SUR L'OEUVRE.
   63rd Divisional Signals are laying a line from 188 Inf. Bde to 72nd Brigade RFA,HQ.

5. At zero plus 30 mins., 1 18-pdr battery 72nd Bde RFA crosses the river and moves forward in close support of 188 Inf. Bde.
   As soon as batteries reach 7,000 yards range on barrage, the remainder 72nd Bde will commence advancing to positions about G.10.b. or G.4.a. in support of 188th Inf. Bde.
   This brigade will cross the canal by bridge F.29.b.7.5.
   72nd Bde RFA will detail advance sections to work in close liaison with each attacking battalion of 188 Inf. Bde.
   When first objective has been taken, one section 315 Bde RFA will advance in close support of 57th Division, under instructions issued by CRA., 57th Division.
   Further advance of Brigades will be ordered as situation developes and wagon lines will be at an half hours notice to move from zero plus 3 hours onwards.
   On the 72nd Bde moving, 315 Bde will come directly under this Office.

6. Each brigade will detail one O.P. to act as Brigade O.P. Once this has been established, battery O.Ps will be established as soon as possible.
   Every effort must be made to push O.Ps forward to newly captured ground without delay. Visual and a combination of telephone and visual communication must be used to the fullest possible extent and arrangements made to supplement telephone communication by all other available means.
   It is hoped to issue 4 pigeons to each brigade. These will be disposed as Brigade Commanders consider best, so that information can be got back in event of communications being down.

7. Co-operation with R.A.F. will be as laid down in XVII Corps Artillery Instructions No.2.
   Brigades must erect their Wireless as soon as possible after a move and put out ground signals.
   Code Ground Signals at present in force are :-
      9th Bde RFA.   A I
      56th Bde RFA,   A II
      72nd Bde RFA,   B III
      315th Bde RFA,   B IV
   GF Calls will be answered by two 18-pdr. batteries and one 4.5" How. battery of 9th Bde Group, till completion of advance of 72nd Bde.
   On arrival in action, after advance, of 72nd Bde RFA, it will detail one 18-pdr and one 4.5" How. battery to answer GF Calls and 9th Bde Group 1 18pdr battery

2/-

Each brigade will detail one Officers' Patrol to go out and get in touch with the situation.

Only one patrol from 9th Bde Group will be out at a time.

Importance of getting their information back to Brigade and D.A. must be impressed on these Officers.

In addition, O.Ps must report all the information they can get, and look-out men will be sent up to assist observing Officers in keeping a general watch on the situation.

All enemy movement will be engaged at once by visual observation.

On no account is the enemy to be allowed to show himself above ground unmolested.

Ammunition re-filling point for 52nd D.A. Group will be F.25.B. situation permits

Arrangements for supplies and water will be as at present until situation permits of watering at the Canal.

Headquarters of formations at Zero hour will be as under :-
```
63rd Div: H.Q.        L.10.d.9.3.
188, 189, & 190 Inf. Bdes.  MONT SUR L'OEUVRE.
57th Div: H.Q.        F.15.c.0.2.
170 Inf. Bde         F.19.c.6.1.
171 Inf. Bde         F.21.b.C.2.
172 Inf. Bde         F.22.b.7.2.
52nd DAHQ.           CANTAING MILL.
```

S.O.S. lines after attack will be the line of the protective barrage.

Watches will be synchronised from this Headquarters.

F.A. Brigades to ACKNOWLEDGE.

                                                          Captain R.A.
                              Brigade Major R.A., 52nd Division.

Issued at 1550.
7th October 1918.

Distribution.

```
Copies No.   1/5    9th Bde RFA
             6/10   56th Bde RFA.
             11/15  72nd Bde RFA.
             16/20  315th Bde RFA.
             21     Staff Captain.
             22     R.O.,R.A.
             23     R.A. Signals.
             24     217th Coy. A.S.C.
             25     52nd D.A.C.
             26     52nd D.T.M.O.
             27     63rd D.A.
             28     57th D.A.
             29/30  War Diary
             31     File.
```

S E C R E T.   OFFICE REFERENCE T.S.261.
                                                TRAIN CIRCULAR No. 78.
                                                FRENCH TRANSPORT No.W.325
STRATEGICAL MOVE OF 52nd DIVISIONAL ARTILLERY
FROM THIRD ARMY TO FIRST ARMY.

Entraining programme.

Entraining station.   **Detraining station.**

A. FREMICOURT   A. ACQ
B. VELU   B. ECURIE

Train No. From stations A.	Train No. From stations B.	UNITS.	Date 1918	Marche	Time of Dept.
1	-	'A' Bty of No.1 Bde.1 G.S.Wgn & 4 lmbd.ammn.wgns.& teams of No.1 Section D.A.C.	20/10	T.55	11.45
-	2	'A' Bty of No.2 Bde.1 G.S.Wgn & 4 lmbd.ammn.wgns & teams of No.2 Section D.A.C.	"	T.56	12.15
3	-	'B' Bty of No.1 Bde.1 G.S.Wgn & 4 lmbd.ammn.wgns & teams of No.1 Section D.A.C.	"	T.58	14.45
-	4	'B' Bty of No.2 Bde.1 G.S.Wgn & 4 lmbd.ammn.wgns & teams of No.2 Section D.A.C.	"	T.59	15.15
5	-	H.Q.R.A., H.Q.D.A.C.,H.Q.Coy Divisional Train.	"	T.61	17.45
-	6	'C' Bty of No.2 Bde.1 G.S.Wgn & 4 lmbd.ammn.wgns & teams of No.2 Section D.A.C.	"	T.62	18.15
7	-	'C' Bty of No.1 Bde.1 G.S.Wgn & 4 lmbd.ammn.wgns & teams of No.1 Section D.A.C.	"	T.64	20.45
-	8	'D' Bty of No.2 Bde.1 G.S.Wgn & 4 lmbd.ammn.wgns & teams of No.2 Section D.A.C.	"	T.65	21.15
9	-	'D' Bty of No.1 Bde.1 G.S.Wgn & 4 lmbd.ammn.wgns & teams of No.1 Section D.A.C.	"	T.67	23.45
-	10	No.2 Bde H.Q., No.2 Section D.A.C less 4 G.S.Wgns,16 lmbd.ammn.wgns & teams. 'Y' T.M.Bty.	21/10	T.68	0.15
11	-	No. 1 Bde H.Q., No.1 Section D.A.C less 4 G.S.Wgns,16 lmbd.ammn.wgns & teams. 'X' T.M.Bty.	"	T.70	2.45

All trains will be type omnibus, i.e., 1 Coach, 30 Covers, 17 flats.

Traffic Office,   Lieut-Colonel,
   CONTEVILLE,   A.D.R.T.-
      18th October,1918.
                                DISTRIBUTION :-
    5 D.D.R.T.(F),G.H.Q.   3 XVII Corps 'Q'   3 R.O.D.CAMDAS
    2 Q.M.G.,G.H.Q.   1 VI Corps 'Q'   1 R.O.D.VECQUEMONT
    3 First Army 'Q'   5 52nd Divl.Artly.   1 R.O.D.LIGNY
    1 A.D.G.T.(1)   1 A.C.T.A.R.   5 DADRT,GREVILLERS
    2 Third Army 'Q'   2 O.C.,R.O.D.   5 Traffic PERNES
    1 A.D.G.T.(111)   4 Captain HARTOPP

B
527
C
A

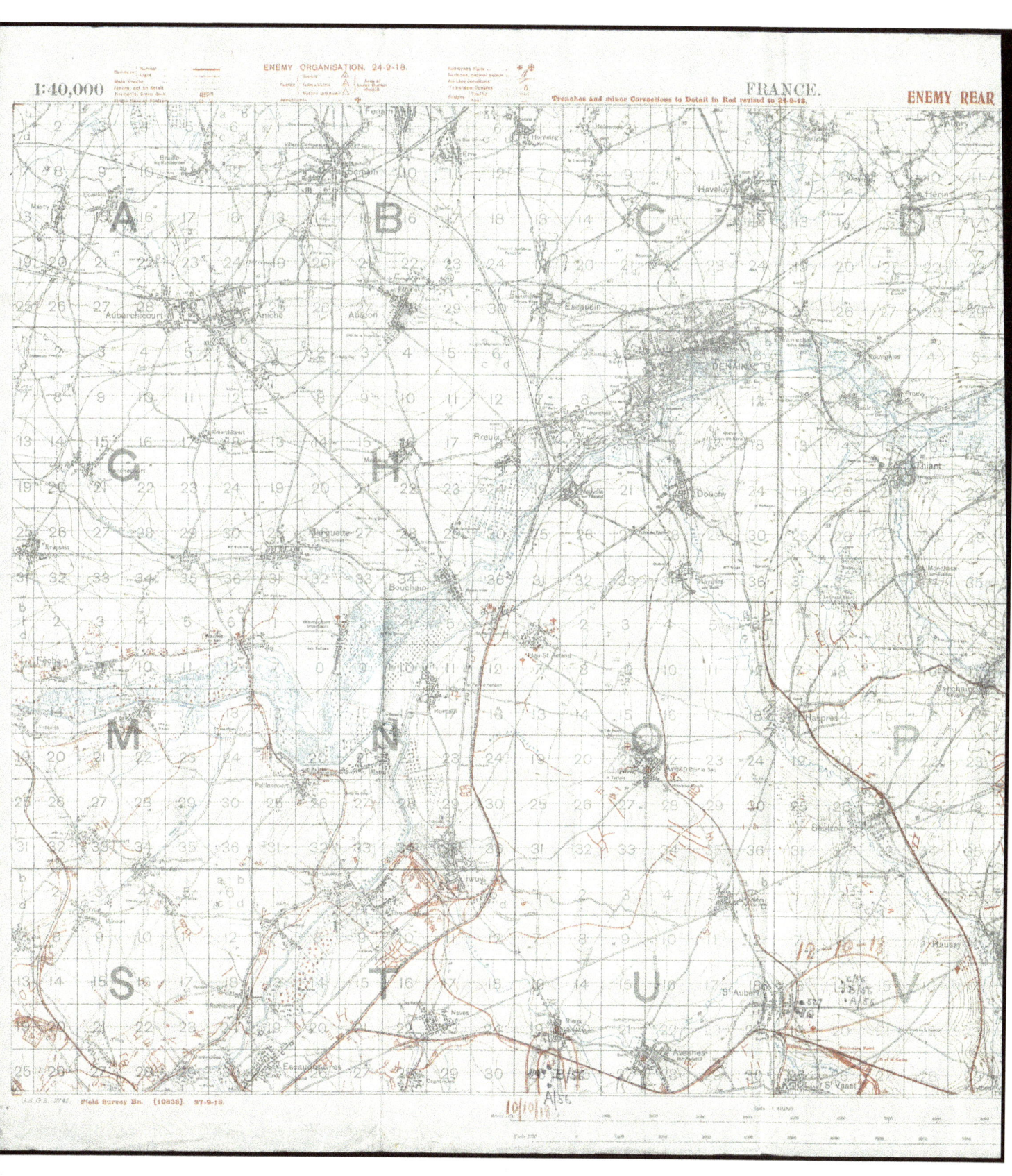

FRANCE. ENEMY REAR ORGANISATION. EDITION 1. a SHEET 51ᴬ

Trenches and minor Corrections to Detail in Red revised to 24-9-18.

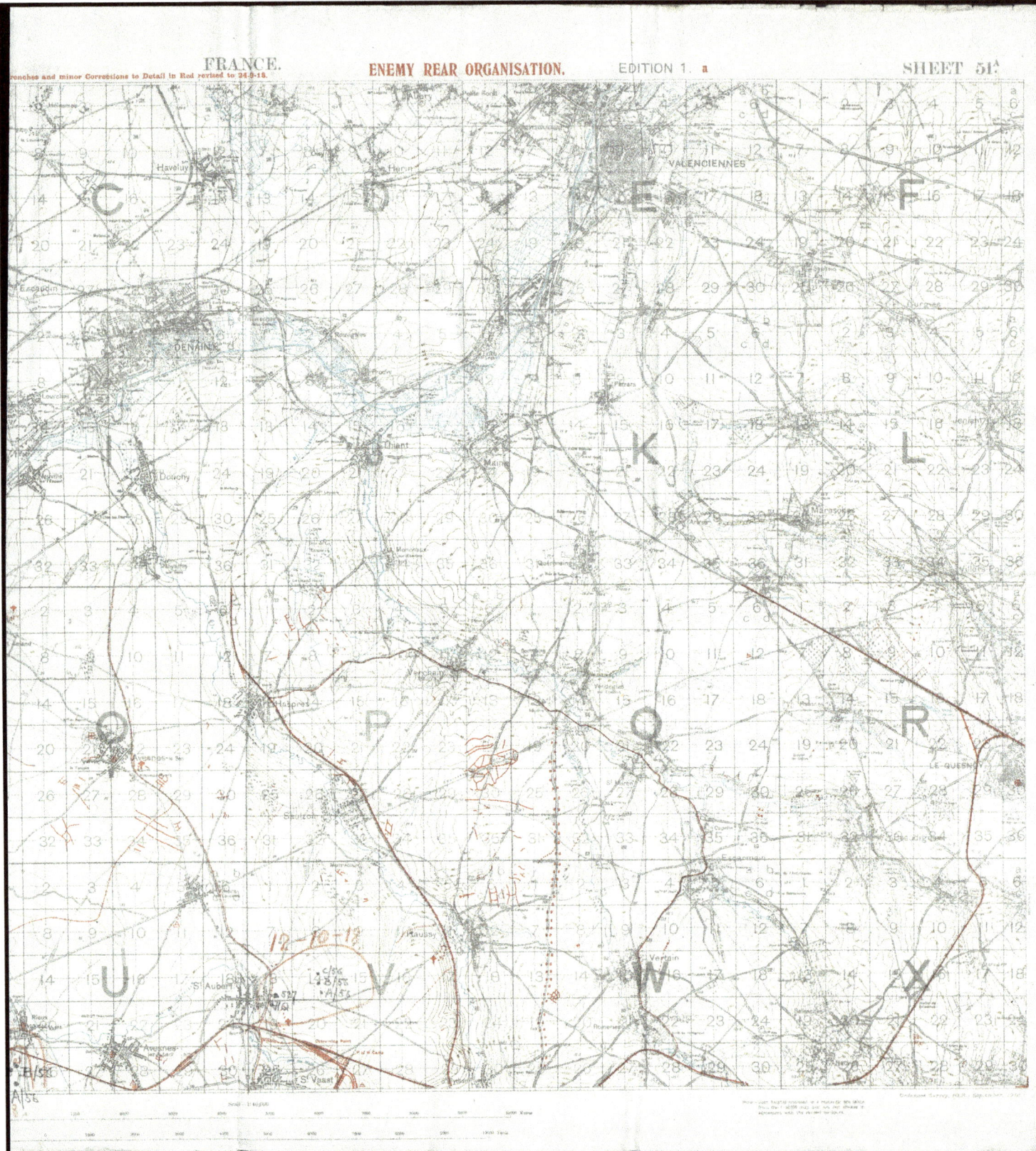

Map III

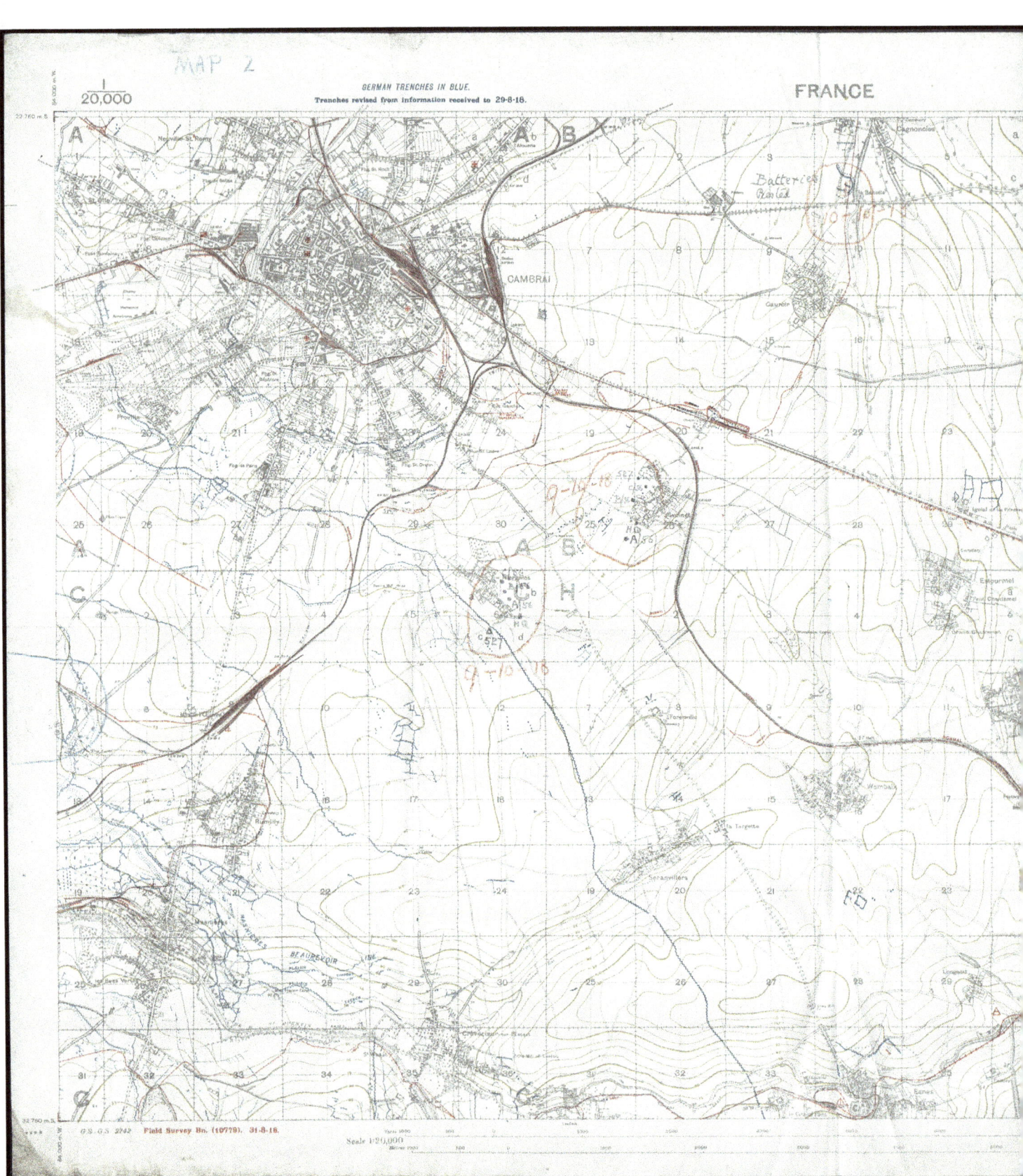

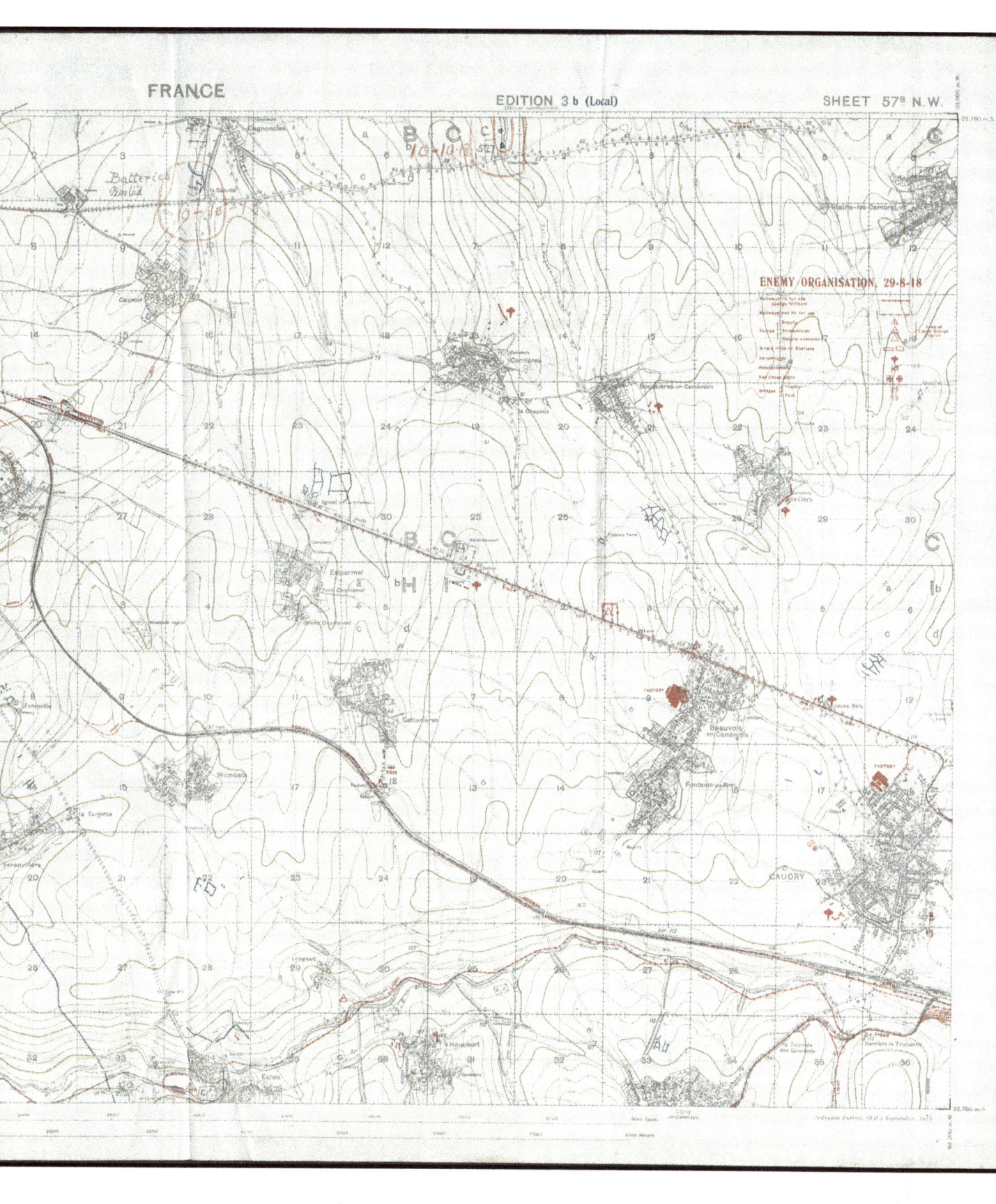

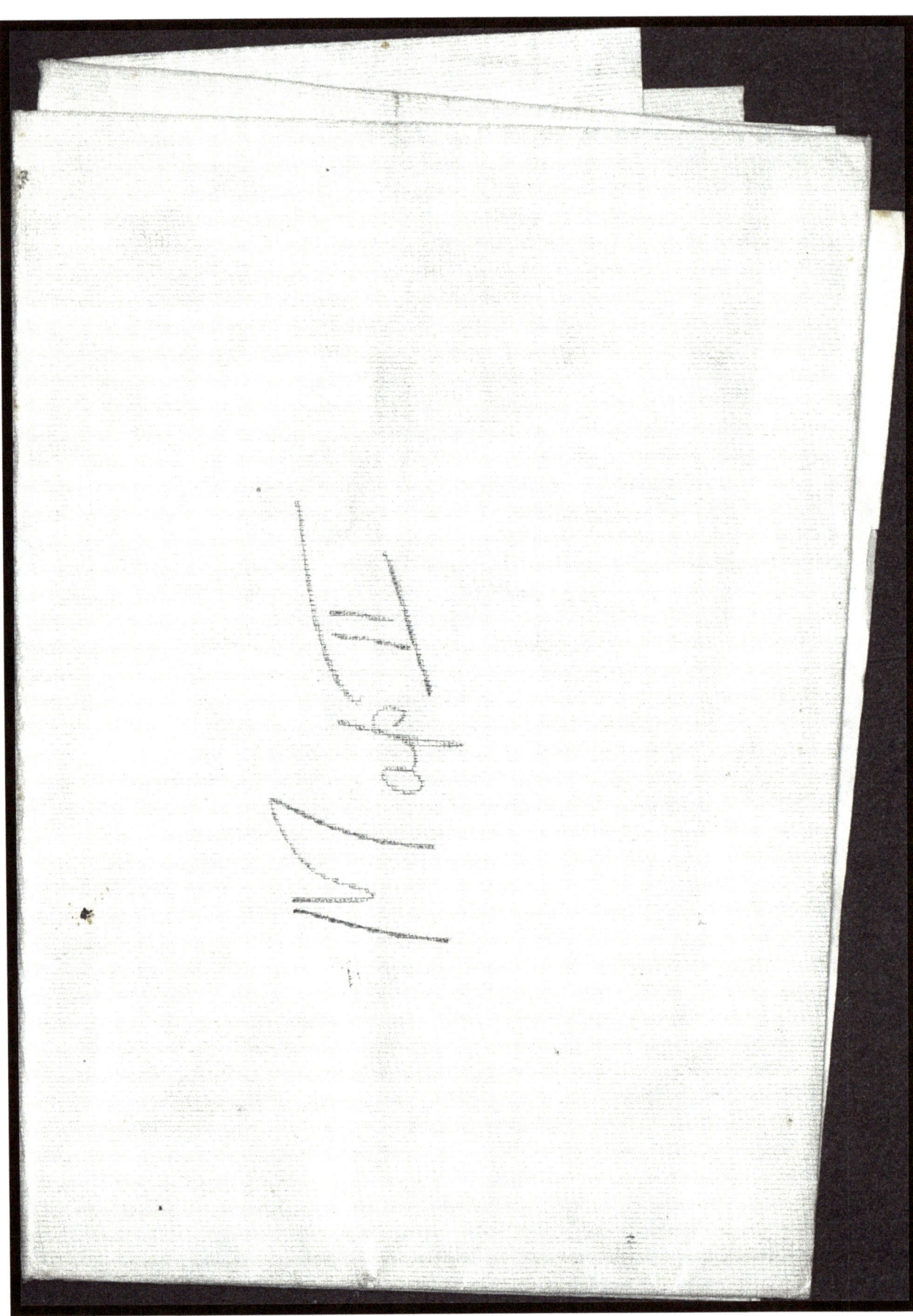

FRANCE. EDITION 7 b. (Local) (With minor detail corrections). SHEET 57c N.E.

Scale 1 : 20,000

Map I

Map I

On His Majesty's Service.

Confidential

Officer I/c A. G.'s Office
at the Base.

CONFIDENTIAL.

WAR DIARY
of
56th Brigade, R.F.A.

From:- 1st November, 1918   To:- 30th November, 1918

(VOLUME IV, Part XI)

a/Lieut.Colonel, R.F.A.
Commanding 56th Brigade, R.F.A.

WAR DIARY
or
INTELLIGENCE SUMMARY.
(Erase heading not required.)

Army Form C. 2118.

56" Brigade RFA
Vol IV Part II

Place	Date	Hour	Summary of Events and Information	Remarks and references to Appendices
Nouex la SAMIAND	1st		Brigade ordered to relieve 63rd Brigade RFA & marched to SAMIAND neighbourhood. see Map IV & Appendix I. Capt R.A. Archer RFA attd to Brigade & attached A/56	Appendix I
Mott du TROY	2nd		Brigade relieved 63rd Brigade RFA in support of 52nd Div 156 Inf Brigade in line (Map IV) Capt BRITTEN posted to B/56	JU
	3rd		N.L "F Watr" posted to Brigade to A/56	JU
	4th		N.L	Th.9
	5th			
	6th			
	7th		Gen Main inspected wagon lines	
	8th		Advanced as in Map I in support of 156 Bde	JU
Bon Secours	9th		Advanced in support of 156 Inf Bde Map IV	JU App II
After lines	10		Advanced in support of 156 Inf Brigade to HERCHIES see Map IV. B abberies in action. The following casualties A/56 172799 Gr Birkett Killed 123220 2/B: Jeffries wounded 43249 D: Fair Trotter wounded 1/10631 D: Howerks wounded 60384 Gr Gooden wounded 92018 D. Gawen wounded	Th.9 App III

Confidential

Army Form C. 2118.

56th Brigade RFA
Vol IV Part XI

WAR DIARY
INTELLIGENCE SUMMARY
(Erase heading not required.)

Place	Date	Hour	Summary of Events and Information	Remarks and references to Appendices
Hechies	10.		2830 Bt. Barn wounded 270211 Gr. Honman wounded	JW
			162982 Dr. Neagal wounded 1678851 Dr. Rees wounded	App IV
			78051 Dr. Thompson wounded 908801 Bt. Greece wounded	
			Still Shock 205214 Dr. Baynall wounded	
			C/56 13437 Dr. Fairweather Killed in action	
			527 66647 Bt. Both wounded 259616 Gr. Davis wounded	
			249067 Bt. Jones wounded Signaller Cpl Wood head wounded	JW
			4 Sapper Scott wounded	JW
	11		B/56 to Erbaut see Map V	JW
			Ammis Lee	
	12		6 Gunners received as reinforcements	JW
	13		Headquarters + 527 Battery to ERBAUT see Map V	JW
	14/6		N.L	
ERBAUT	15			
	17		B/56 taken off SOS line call Batteries out of action	JW
			6 3 horses received from 12" D.A. Lt Brown R.F.A. posted	JW
			to A/56 C Battery to COLROY	JW
	18		A Battery to SERAULT	JW
			9 driver reinforcements received	JW
	19-22		N.L	JW
	23.		27 Gunners 1 Corporal 1 Bdr. + 3 Dr. Reinforcements	JW

Confidential

56th Bde RFA Army Form C. 2118.

WAR DIARY
INTELLIGENCE SUMMARY.
Vol IV Part II

(Erase heading not required.)

Place	Date	Hour	Summary of Events and Information	Remarks and references to Appendices
ERBAUT	24-9/6 28-11		Nil	Jul / Jul / Jul
	29-11		Major N M de la P Beresford Peirse to be B.M. 39th D.A. & struck off strength accordingly	
	30-11		Nil	

Th Ingratt Lt Col
Comdg 56th Brigade
RFA

Appendices
to
War Diary
for
month of
November.

56th Bde. R.F.A.

Appendix I

SECRET.   Copy No.

                    52nd DIVISIONAL ARTILLERY ORDER NO. 47

        Reference map 1/40000
                Sheets 44 and 44a.

1.   52nd Divisional Artillery will relieve 12th Divisional Artillery
between November 1st and 3rd.

2.   9th Brigade R.F.A. will relieve 63rd Brigade R.F.A. in the line
under orders of 12th Divisional Artillery.
        9th Brigade R.F.A. will move up into Divisional Reserve, relieving
the 62nd Brigade R.F.A.
        D.A.Cs. will relieve each other.

3.   Details of the approach march are given in the attached March
table.
        Usual distance will be maintained on the march.

4.   Train Wagons of No.2 Section D.A.C. and 58th Brigade R.F.A. will
accompany units on 1st, loaded with rations for the 2nd.
        Remainder 217th Coy A.S.C. will relieve No.3 Coy, 12th Divl.Train
at LANDAS on November 2nd, after delivery of rations for the 3rd, under
arrangements between Coy.Commanders concerned.
        Rations for the 4th will be delivered to 9th Brigade Headquarters
and No.1 Section D.A.C. after their arrival in new area on the 3rd.

5.   52nd D.A.H.Q. will assume command of the artillery covering 52nd
Division at 1200 hours 3rd instant.

6.   52nd Divisional Artillery to ACKNOWLEDGE.

                                        W.G.Harriss
                                                Captain R.A.,
31st October 1915.   Brigade Major R.A.,52nd Division.

DISTRIBUTION -

            Copies No.1/5   9th Brigade R.F.A.
                     6/10   58th Brigade R.F.A.
                    11/13   52nd D.A.C.
                       14   217th Coy. A.S.C.
                       15   52nd Division "Q"
                       16   12th D.A.
                       17   R.A.,VIII Corps.
                       18   52nd Division "G"
                       19   D.A.P.M. 52nd Div.
                       20   R.A.Sigs.
                       21   D.G.R.A.
                       22   R.O.R.A.
                    23/24   War Diary.
                       25   File.

MARCH TABLE.

Serial No.	Date.	Unit.	From.	To.	Route.	Remarks.
1.	Nov. 1st.	56th Bde RFA.	MAZINGHEM	BOSULT Pen.	FLINES – COUTICHES – ORCHIES. To be clear of FLINES by 1030 and NOT to enter ORCHIES before 1045.	Take over Wagon Lines vacated morning 1st by 62nd Bde RFA.
2.		No.2 Sect. D.A.C.	FRAIS MARAIS.	F.B.d. West of RUMEGIES.	FLINES – ORCHIES – LANDAS – VIEUX CONDE. To follow 56th Brigade and to be clear of FLINES before 1100.	Take over Wagon Lines No.1 Sect. 12th D.A.C.
3.	Nov. 2nd.	5th Bde RFA.	ROSULT area	Line	Route as ordered by 12th D.A.	Relieves 63rd Brigade in Line but remains in 62nd Brigade RFA Wagon Lines.
4.	Nov. 3rd.	8th Bde RFA.	MAZIERES.	ROSULT area.	No.2 FLINES – ORCHIES and to be clear of ORCHIES by 1015.	Takes over Wagon Lines vacated morning 3rd by 63rd Brigade RFA.
5.	Nov. 3rd.	H.Q. and No.1 Sect. D.A.C.	FRAIS MARAIS.	ROSULT area.	FLINES – ORCHIES to follow 8th Bde RFA and to be clear of FLINES by 1105.	Take over Wagon Lines vacated morning 3rd by Headquarters and No.2 Section, 12th D.A.C.

SECRET.   Copy No.

                    12th Divisional Artillery Order No. 130.
                    ──

Reference Map - 1/40,000
    Sheets 44 and 44A.   31st October, 1918.

1.   12th Divisional Artillery will be relieved by the 52nd Divisional
Artillery between November 1st. and November 3rd. in accordance with
Table A., attached.

2. (a) Details regarding relief in the Line on 2nd November of 63rd
Brigade by 56th Brigade R.F.A. to be arranged between Brigade
Commanders concerned.
    (b) Command of Batteries will pass when the relief of the Battery
is complete.
         Command of the Group will pass to O.C. 56th Brigade R.F.A.
when the relief of the 63rd Brigade is complete.
    (c) Completion of the relief will be reported by wire.
    (d) O.C. 63rd Brigade will arrange to have one Officer per
Battery with relieving Battery 56th Brigade until such time as O.C.
Battery 56th Brigade considers he no longer requires him.

3. (a) All telephone lines, S.O.S. Rockets, etc. will be handed over. $\frac{1}{20000}$
Maps will be handed over as follows -
         63rd Brigade to 56th Brigade.
         62nd Brigade will send all 1/20,000 maps to 12th D.A.H.Q.
             before marching out on 1st prox.
    (b) 12th Divisional Artillery units will march out with all
Echelons full.

4.   Units 12th Divisional Artillery will take over billets in the
Rest Area from the 52nd Divisional Artillery units
as follows - 62 Bde. from 56 Bde - 63 Bde from 9 Bde - 12 DAC from 52 DAC.
5. (a) March of units to FRAIS MARAIS AREA will be in accordance with
Table A.
   (b) Usual "distances" will be maintained on the march.

6.   Lorries to convey Trench Mortar Batteries will be at 12th D.A.
H.Q., SAMEON at 8.30 a.m. on Nov. 3rd, where guide from T.M.
Batteries will meet them.

7.   277th Army Brigade R.F.A. will not be relieved until a later
date. It will come under tactical control of O.C. 56th Brigade
R.F.A. on his assuming command of the Group.

8.   Command of the Field Artillery covering 52nd Division will pass
to G.R.A., 52nd Division, at 12.00 on 3rd November, at which hour
12th D.A. H.Q. will close at SAMEON and open at W 12 b 9 2.

9.   12th Divisional Artillery units to acknowledge.

                                            Hugh Walker
                                                 Major,
                                       Brigade Major 12th D. A.

Copy No. 1. 62 Bde. R.F.A. (4 spare)
         2. 63 Bde. R.F.A. (4 spare)   9.   No. 1 Coy. Train.
         3. 277 Bde. R.F.A.   10. VIII Corps R.A.
         4. 12th D.A.C.   (2 spare)   11. 12th Divn. (G).
         5. 12th D.T.M.O.   12. 12th Divn. (Q).
         6. O.C. V/12 T.M.B.   13. 52nd Divn. (G)
         7. 12th D.A. Signals.   14. 52nd D. A. (3 spare)
         8. Staff Capt., RA.   15. A.P.M., VIII Corps.
             16. D.A.P.M., 52nd Division.
             17. 156th Inf. Bde.
             18. 67th Brigade R.G.A.
             19 - 22. War Diary and File.

S E C R E T.

TABLE A.

Issued with 12th Divisional Artillery Order No. 130.

Serial No.	Date	Unit	From	To	Starting Point and hour of passing.	Route	Remarks
1.	Nov. 1st	62 Bde. RFA	ROSULT Area	56 Bde's Billets WAZIERES	Cross road O 2 b 2 8 10.15	BEUVRY - BOUVIGNIES - FLINES - RACHES.	Not to enter FLINES before 11.00
2.	Nov. 1st	No. 1 Section D.A.C.	FME DERIS	FRAIS MARAIS H 12 c	To march so as to be clear of ORCHIES by 10.45	LANDAS - ORCHIES - FLINES - RACHES	Not to enter FLINES before 11.30.
3.	Nov. 2nd	63 Bde. RFA	Action	Wagon Lines on relief by 56 Bde. RFA.	Relief to be carried out by daylight. Sections to move East on N.& S. line thro' LECELIES at 20 mins. interval	Movement East by road through I 30 a & b, J 25 and J 26. Movement West by roads J 33, J 32, J 31 and I 36.	
4.	Nov. 2nd	56 Bde. RFA	Wagon Lines	Action	As possible with regard to refilling.		
5.	Nov. 2nd	No. 1 Coy. Train	LANDAS	WAZIERES		BEUVRY - BOUVIGNIES - FLINES.	
6.	Nov. 3rd	63 Bde. RFA	ROSULT Area	9 Bde's Billets WAZIERES	Level crossing C 2 a 2 1 at 10.00	BEUVRY - BOUVIGNIES - FLINES.	Not to enter FLINES before 11.00
7.	Nov. 3rd	H.Q. and No. 2 Section, D.A.C.	ROSULT Area	FRAIS MARAIS	Level crossing C 2 a 2 1 at 11.00.	As above.	

5th Brigade, R.F.A.

B.M./25.B/45.2/54.
557 Bty.Battery

Reference Blst. Warder No.47.

Brigade will march to L.of C. Area to-morrow 1st instant, and will take over Waggon Lines as follows.

Bat. kept by   1/20.

    Hqurs.   A.18.a.5.5.
    'A' Bty. I.6.a.8.5.
    'B' "   I.25.a.5.9.
    'C' "   I.35.c.5.7.
    527 "   I.20.c.5.4.

Starting Point 'A' Bty. Horse Lines.

Order of March Hd.Qrs. 'A', 'B', 'C' and 557 Batteries.

    'A' Bty. pass Starting Point 0830 hrs.
    'B' "   "   "   0835 "
    'C' "   "   "   0840 "
    557 "   "   "   0845 "

Following distances in supersession of all previous orders
    100 yards between Batteries.

Batteries will march closed up with no distances between Sections.

All transport except one Cook's Cart and one Water Cart per Battery and one Cook's Cart and one Maltese Cart for Headquarters will march 100 yards in rear of 557 Battery under an officer to be detailed by O.C. 557 Battery, the necessary N.C.O's being detailed by Batteries for their own transport.

All Battery private vehicles will march in rear of the Brigade under an officer to be detailed by O.C. 'A'/5A Battery. This officer will report for instructions at 0830 hrs. to the O.C. Brigade at the Starting Point.

Batteries will obtain the time from the Adjutant before moving off. Special attention must be paid to pulling out clear of roadway two minutes before halts.

Batteries will send on the usual advanced parties independently. All Battery cyclists will accompany advanced parties.

Brigade will probably be increased by three batteries in the course of the march.

ACKN. R.14.58.

31st October, 1918.   Adjutant 5th Bde. R.F.A.

S E C R E T.   12 D.A. No. R.A. 1075/1.

63rd Brigade ~~Group~~ R.F.A.
56th Brigade, R.F.A. Group (2 copies)
67th Brigade, R.G.A.

App;*

Reference this office No. R.A.1075 of to-day.

1. The Northern boundary of the Corps will run from I 18 a 8 8 to about J 10 c 0 0 - J 10 b 9 6 - along N.E. bank of ESCAUT FLEUVE and JARD CANAL (inclusive) to K 19 b 7 9 - thence the VERGNE River (exclusive), and not as stated in para. 1 (b).

2. Consequent on above there will be no taking over necessary from any troops of 58th Division.

[signature]
Major,
Brigade Major 12th D.A.

2nd Novr., 1918.

"C" Form.
MESSAGES AND SIGNALS.

Army Form C. 2123.
(In books of 100.)

No. of Message _____

Prefix _____ Code 530 Words 31
Received From 136 Bde By Scott
Sent, or sent out. At ___ m To ___ m By ___
Office Stamp Su 2/11/18

Charges to Collect

Service Instructions 1EB

Handed in at _____ Office _____ m. Received 3.45 m

TO 56th Bde RFA

*Sender's Number	Day of Month.	In reply to Number	AAA
BM111	2		

Ref No RA1075 of date aaa Northern boundary altered to J18A88 J10c00 J10B96, thence along JARD canal and VERONE river

FROM PLACE & TIME 12th Divl Arty

* This line should be erased if not required

SECRET.   12 D.A. No. R.A. 1075.

Ref: Map - 1/40,000.

63rd Brigade Group R.F.A. (1 spare)
56th Brigade, R.F.A.
67th Brigade, R.G.A.

1.   The boundary of the VIII Corps from 0600, November 3rd, will run -
   (a) On South.
   From Q 9 c 2 4 - Q 16 c 9 5 - R 13 c 5 4 - R 20 a 1 1 - R 9 c 9 1 - thence along HAISNE River.
   (b) On North.
   From J 8 d 9 4 - J 10 a 5 9 - along N. and E. bank ESCAUT FLEUVE and JARD CANAL (inclusive) to K 19 b 7 9 - thence the VERGNE River (exclusive).
   (c) The Inter-Divisional boundary will run -
   From HAUTE RIVE J 36 b 4 5 - Q 3 b 5 9 - K 28 d 1 2 - L'ECARLATE (L 25 a 5 7).

2.   Consequent on above, 156th Inf. Bde. is to extending its front, taking over from 8th Division (23rd Inf. Bde., 2nd W. Yorks Regt.) on Right, and from 58th Division (174th Inf. Bde., 8th London Regt.) on Left.   Relief to be completed by 0600 Novr. 3rd.
   Details are being arranged direct between Inf. Bde's concerned.

3.   O.C. 63rd Brigade Group will arrange in consultation with G.O.C. 156th Inf. Bde. and O.C. 56th Brigade R.F.A. regarding the distribution of the Field Artillery to cover the above line, moving any Batteries he considers necessary.

2nd Novr., 1918.

                                                    Major,
                                         Brigade Major 12th D.A.

S E C R E T.   12 D.A. No. R.A. 1075.

Ref. Map - 1/40,000.

63rd Brigade Group R.F.A. (1 spare)
56th Brigade, R.F.A.
67th Brigade, R.G.A.

1. The boundary of the VIII Corps from 0600, November 3rd, will run -
  (a) On South.
  From Q 9 c 2 4 - Q 16 c 9 5 - R 13 c 5 4 - R 20 a 1 1 - R 9 c 9 1 - thence along HAISNE River.
  (b) On North.
  From J 8 d 9 4 - J 10 a 5 9 - along N. and E. bank ESCAUT FLEUVE and JARD CANAL (inclusive) to K 19 b 7 9 - thence the VERGNE River (exclusive).
  (c) The inter-Divisional boundary will run -
  From HAUTE RIVE J 36 b 4 5 - Q 3 b 5 9 - K 28 d 1 2 - L'ECARLATE (L 25 a 5 7).

2. Consequent on above, 156th Inf. Bde. is to extending its front, taking over from 8th Division (23rd Inf. Bde., 2nd W. Yorks Regt.) on Right, and from 56th Division (174th Inf. Bde., 8th London Regt.) on Left. Relief to be completed by 0600 Novr. 3rd.
    Details are being arranged direct between Inf. Bde's concerned.

3. O.C. 63rd Brigade Group will arrange in consultation with G.O.C. 156th Inf. Bde. and O.C. 56th Brigade R.F.A. regarding the distribution of the Field Artillery to cover the above line, moving any Batteries he considers necessary.

2nd Novr., 1918.

Hugh Walker
Major,
Brigade Major 12th D.A.

To O.C.

A/63rd BRIGADE.
B/63rd BRIGADE.
C/63rd BRIGADE.
D/63rd BRIGADE.
277th BRIGADE A.F.A.
FILE.

4 copies

SECRET.

The following S.O.S. Lines will come into force at 06.00 hours 3/11/18.-

63rd Bde. R.F.A.

A/63 .... K.36.b.4.5. to K.36.b.30.85.
B/63 .... J.12.c.4.0. to J.12.c.0.7.
C/63 .... Swinging Battery superimposed on B/63.
D/63 .... 2 Hows. on Bridge J.18.d.8.9
         2 Hows. - Lock - J.12.c.6.7
         2 Hows. - Crossing K.13.d.22.35

277th Brigade A.F.A.

18-pdr Line... K.34.a.9.5.
           K.27.c.6.6.
4.5" Hows.... 2 Hows. - Pont de la Vernette K.26.b.6.6.
           2 Hows. - Crossing K.27.d.4.1
           2 Hows. - Crossing K.34.a.35.40

Reference our S.616. - S.O.S Sectors.

These will now be as follows -
(1) K.34.a.9.5. to K.33.b.7.9.
(2) K.33.b.7.9. to K.27.c.6.6.
(3) K.36.b.4.5. to K.36.b.30.85.
(4) J.12.c.4.0. to J.12.c.0.7.

2nd November, 1918.

Adjutant, 63rd Brigade R.F.A.

In use 06.00 3/11

SECRET.   Copy No......6......

52nd DIVISIONAL ARTILLERY ORDER NO. 50.

App 1**

1. 52nd Division are taking over the whole 8th Corps front, the 157th Infantry Brigade relieving the 23rd Infantry Brigade on the night 4/5th November.

2. Consequent upon the above relief, the 33rd and 45th Brigades R.F.A. of the 8th D.A. come under orders of C.R.A. 52nd Division at 0800, 5th instant.

3. 16th and 87th Brigades R.G.A. will also be affiliated to the 52nd Division.

4. 33rd Brigade R.F.A. will be in liaison with 157th Infantry Brigade and will arrange Battalion liaison in direct consultation with G.O.C., 157th Infantry Brigade.
   56th Brigade R.F.A. will remain in liaison with 156th Infantry Bde.
   9th Brigade R.F.A. will be under direct control of this office, but, as they also are covering the 156th Bde. front, O.C., 56th Brigade R.F.A. may call on them direct for fire if he wishes to.
   45th Brigade R.F.A. will remain in Divisional Reserve.

5. S.O.S. lines will remain as before unless the G.O.C. Infantry Bde. wishes them altered, when the necessary modifications will be made and reported to this office.

6. The northern Divisional Boundary will be -
   I.18.c.3.3. - J.10.c.0.0. - J.10.c.9.3. along North East Bank of ESCAUT FLEUVE and JARD CANAL (inclusive) to K.18.b.7.9. and thence the VERGNE River (exclusive).
   Southern Divisional Boundary will be -
   Q.9.c.2.4. - Q.16.c.9.3. - R.13.c.3.4. - R.20.a.1.1. - R.9.c.9.1. thence along HAISNE River.
   Boundary between 9th and 33rd Brigades R.F.A.
       Line Q.4.central - K.35.central.
   Boundary between 9th and 56th Brigades R.F.A.
       Line K.20.a.0.0. - K.16.c.0.0.
   Boundary between Heavy and Field Artillery.
       Line K.14.b.5.0. - K.22.c.7.7. - R.3.central - R.10.d.0.0.

   Within these boundaries Brigades will be prepared to answer GF calls with 2-18-pdr and 1 - 4.5" how. Batteries.
       LL calls will be answered by all Batteries that can bear, irrespective of zones.
       NF calls will also be answered in those zones and 4.5" How. Batteries will be prepared to answer ANF Calls as well within the Bde zone.
       During counter preparations GF calls will only be answered by a section of the Batteries detailed.
       During S.O.S., G.F. calls will not be answered by Field Artillery and LL calls by 1 section only of all Batteries that can bear.
       Rates of fire for GF and LL calls will be 3 minutes INTENSE.
       The wireless receiving set from D.A.H.Q. will be sent to 9th Brigade R.F.A. for use with forward section D/69th Battery R.F.A.

7. The Divisional policy will be to keep close touch with the enemy by active patrolling and follow up any withdrawal as laid down in 52nd D.A. Order No. 49.

8. F.A. Brigades to ACKNOWLEDGE.

                                          [signature]
                                                Captain R.A.,
4th November, 1918.   Brigade Major R.A., 52nd Division.
Distribution :- as over

DISTRIBUTION :-

Copies No. 1/5   9th Bde RFA.
         6/10 56th Brigade RFA.
         11/15 33rd Brigade RFA.
         16/20 45th Brigade RFA.
         21   52nd D.A.C.
         22   9th D.A.
         23   56th D.A.
         24   4? D.D.?
         25   52nd Division "G"
         26   155 Infantry Brigade.
         27   156 Infantry Brigade.
         28   157 Infantry Brigade.
         29   H.A., 6th Corps.
         30   H.A., 8th Corps.
         31   87th Brigade R.G.A.
         32   16th Brigade R.G.A.
         33   E.C.R.
         34   R.O.R.A.
         35   R.A.Signals.
         36/37 War Diary.
         38   File.

156th. INFANTRY BRIGADE ORDER No. 69.

Copy No. 5

8th. November 1918.

Ref. Map
1/20,000 - Sheet 44 N.E.

1. (a) The enemy has retired East of ANTOING POMMEROEUL CANAL and civilians report that he will not stand there but is retiring further East.
   (b) VIII Corps Cyclist Bn. have secured the line PERUWELZ - BONSECOURS - LORETTE and met no opposition.
   (c) 157th. Inf. Bde. on right are on CONDE PERUWELZ Road.

2. The 156th. Inf. Bde. and affiliated troops will advance tomorrow (9/11/18) and secure the line of the ANTOING POMMEROEUL CANAL between F.21.D.5.2 and G.15.C.6.5.

3. (a) An Advance Guard consisting of 7th. Royal Scots, "C" Coy. 52nd. Bn. M.G.C., "A" Battery, 56th. Bde. R.F.A. and 1 Section 156th. L.T.M. Battery under command of Lieut. Col. W.T. EWING, D.S.O., will cover the advance of the Bde. and will make good the following lines:-
   (a) CONDE - PERUWELZ Railway between L.7.A.7.5 and L.25.A.9.6.
   (b) PERUWELZ - CONDE Road between L.3.A.2.7 and L.21.B.7.6
   (c) CADROUILLET - OUTREL'EAU - LENOUVEAU MONDE - High ground in L.12.C - L.19.central.
   (b) Reports will be rendered when these lines have been reached and when touch has been gained on the right flank.
   (c) In view of fact that Northern flank will probably be exposed throughout the day, Advance Guard Commander will arrange for 1 Coy. of his Main Guard to march along the FOLQUIN - PERUWELZ Road.
   (d) The Advance Guard will move forward from present line (K.29.central - K.16.central) at 0615.
   (e) O.C., "A" Battery, 56th. Bde. R.F.A., will report to O.C., 7th. Royal Scots (K.22.D.2.5) at 0500 to receive instructions.

4. The Main Body will march along the HERGNIES - MONT DE PERUWELZ - BONSECOURS Road in accordance with attached march table.

5. Advance will be pressed as rapidly as possible. If crossing of the ANTOING CANAL is in any way possible 4th. Royal Scots will be prepared to pass through 7th. Royal Scots and make good the Eastern Bank.

6. First Line Transport will march with units, Lewis Gun limbers in rear of Coys. remainder in rear of Battalions.

7. Reports to head of Main Body.

8. ACKNOWLEDGE.

Sayer
Captain,
Brigade Major, 156th. Inf. Bde.

Issued at 0010

Copy No. 1 to 4th. R.S.	No. 8 to "C" Coy. 52 MG Bn.	No. 15 174 I.B.
2 5th. R.S.	9 O.C. Bearer Pty.	16 175 I.B.
	1/1 L.F.A.	
3 7th. S.R.	10 1/2 L.F.A.	17 S.C.
4 156th. L.T.M.By	11 410 Fld. Co. R.E.	18 B.T.O.
5 56th. Bde. R.F.A.	12 412 Fld. Co. R.E.	19 Sigs.
6 "A" By. 56th. RFA	13 52nd. Div.	20 & 21 Diary
7 "B" Co. 52 M.G.Bn	14 157th. Inf. Bde.	22 File

SECRET.   Copy No......6.

52nd DIVISIONAL ARTILLERY ORDER NO. 51.

1. 52nd D.A. Order No. 49 is cancelled.

2. When the enemy withdraws, 52nd Division will follow up to gain and maintain touch with his main forces.

3. (a) The Infantry Brigade in the Right Section, with one affiliated M.G. Company, will cross the ESCAUT and JARD Canal and make good the general line Q.6.a. - K.29.central.
   (b) The Infantry Brigade in the Left Section, with two affiliated M.G. Companies, will cross the ESCAUT and JARD Canal and make good the general line K.29.central - K.16.central.

4. (a) The 8th Corps Cyclist Battalion (less 1 Coy.), will cross immediately in rear of the Left Brigade and push forward and secure the following objectives:-
   (i) VIEUX CONDE. - PERUWELZ Railway (K.1, L.31, L.25, L.19, L.13.
   (ii) CONDE - MONT DE PERUWELZ - PERUWELZ Road (L.32, L.26, L.20, L.14, L.8.)
   (iii) CONDE - CR. de L'ERMITAGE - BOQUET Road (L.33, L.27, L.21, L.15, L.8.b. and d.)

   (iv) The line LORETTE - BONSECOURS - PERUWELZ.

5. As soon as the line Q.6 - K.16 has been made good, Infantry Brigades will push on in accordance with para 2.
   Right Infantry Brigade Headquarters will move along the road RIEUX DE CONDE - GD. QUENOY - CHENE RAOUL.
   Left Infantry Brigade Headquarters along the road HERGNIES - MONT-DE-PERUWELZ.

6. At the earliest possible moment the following bridges will be made :-

   (a) Near COUPURE K.27.d.3.1.
       (Bridges HERGNIES "A" and HERGNIES "B")
   (b) Near PONT DE LA VERNETTE.
       (Bridges VERNETTE "X" and VERNETTE "Y")

7. As soon as these bridges are ready, a squadron 4th Hussars will cross and move forward to co-operate with the cyclists.

8. Artillery action in support of the advance will be as follows :-
   (a) As soon as information is received that the enemy has withdrawn, 9th Brigade Batteries west of the River SCARPE will advance to the old 277th Brigade R.F.A. positions about HAUTEVIVE and support the initial advance of the Left Infantry Brigade.
   All arrangements must be made to occupy these positions at short notice in the dark.
   Wagon Lines will in consequence be at an hour's notice to move.
   (b) A/56th Brigade R.F.A. will move forward in close support of the leading troops of the Left Infantry Brigade, with whom it will work in close liaison in rear of the Cavalry and cross the canal.
   56th Brigade R.F.A. (less A Battery) will follow and support the advance of the Left Brigade, working in liaison with the G.O.C. Infantry Brigade.
   (c) 19th Battery R.F.A. will follow the 56th Brigade across the Canal, get into touch with and support the leading Battalion of the Right Infantry Brigade, working in liaison with the Battalion Commander.
   (d) 33rd Brigade R.F.A. will support the advance of the Right Infantry Brigade as long as possible, from present positions.

9. With the exception of the moves detailed in the preceding paragraph units will not move without further orders.

10. The Moves will take place on the code word "HUNT", which will be wired to Brigades and sent by special D.R. to the Wagon Lines Commanders of 9th and 56th Brigades.

11. A central,

- 2 -

11. A central visual station will be established about K.25.d.1.2.

12. D.A.H.Q. will move with Headquarters 52nd Division to MARIE DE NIVELLE as soon as leading Brigade is across the JARD Canal.

13. Artillery Brigades ACKNOWLEDGE.

[signature]
Captain R.A.,
Brigade Major R.A., 52nd Division.

5th November 1918.

DISTRIBUTION -

Copies No.	
1/5	9th Brigade R.F.A.
6/10	56th Brigade R.F.A.
11/15	33rd Brigade R.F.A.
16	D.A.C.
17	155th Inf. Bde.
18.	156th Inf. Bde.
19.	157th Inf. Bde.
20.	52nd Division "G"
21.	8th Corps R.A.
22.	8th Corps H.A.
23.	58th D.A.
24.	3rd C.D.A.
25.	16th Brigade R.G.A.
26.	67th Brigade R.G.A.
27.	S.O.R.A.
28.	R.O.R.A.
29.	R.A. Sigs.
30/31	War Diary.
32.	File.

4th. Royal Scots
7th. Royal Scots
7th. Sco. Rifles
156th. L.T.M. Battery
"B" Coy. 52nd. Bn. M.G.C. (Group Commander)

SECRET.

BM 275

For your information.

With reference to this Office BM 259 of the 5th. inst:-

1. The order in which personnel of units will cross the footbridges when constructed, is as follows:-
   (1) 2 Coys. Right Front Line Bn. and 1 Section M.Gs.
   (2) VIII Corps Cyclist Bn. (less 1 Coy.)
   (3) Support Bn. and 1 Section L.T.M. Battery
   (4) 1 Section 52nd. Bn. M.G.C.
   (5) Right Front Line Bn. (less 2 Coys.)
   (6) Left Front Line Battalion.
   (7) Bde. H.Q. and L.T.M. Battery (less 1 section)

2. As soon as the Pontoon Bridges have been constructed units and transport will cross in the following order:-
   (1) Squadron 4th. Hussars
   (2) 2 Sections 52nd. Bn. M.G.C. with 12 limbers.
   (3) "A" Battery, 56th. Bde. R.F.A.
   (4) 4 Lewis gun limbers, 1 magazine limber and 2 S.A.A. limbers of Support Bn. plus 1 limber L.T.M. Battery.
   (5) 56th. Bde. R.F.A. (less 1 Battery)
   (6) 1 Battery 9th. Bde. R.F.A.
   (7) 1 Coy. 52nd. Bn. M.G.C. with transport
   (8) 1/2nd. Low. Field Ambulance.
   (9) First Line Transport, 156th. Inf. Bde. in following order:-
       (a) Right Front Line Bn.
       (b) Left Front Line Bn.
       (c) Support Bn. (less fighting limbers mentioned in 4 above)
       (d) Bde. H.Q. and L.TM. Battery.

7th. November 1918.

Captain,
Brigade Major, 156th. Inf. Bde.

Copies to:-
157th. Inf. Bde.
52nd. Bn. M.G.C.
56th. Bde. R.F.A. (together with copies of BM 259, 260, 263 & 264)
9th. Bde. R.F.A.
412th. Field Coy. R.E.
1/1st. Low. Fld. Amb.
1/2nd. Low. Fld. Amb.
S.C. (2)
R.T.O.
O.C., Bde. Sigs.
Spare (for Traffic officers) (6)
Diary (2)
File.

SECRET.

BM 259

4th. Royal Scots
7th. Royal Scots
7th. Sco. Rifles
156th. L.T.M. Battery
"B". Coy. 52nd. Bn. M.G.C.
412th. Field Coy. R.E.

Ref. Map 1/40,000 - Sheet 44 (Edition 2)

BM 200 of 29/10/18, BM 233 of 1/11/18 and BM 242 of 2/11/18 are cancelled and the following instructions are substituted:-

1. The present policy on this front is not to push any attack over the JARD CANAL too energetically or at the expense of many lives.

2. An active system of patrolling will, however, be kept up so as to ensure that the enemy does not retire without our knowledge. Patrols will, therefore, be pushed out every night and just before dawn, or after dawn if misty.

3. In the event of it being ascertained that the enemy has retired from the JARD CANAL, the Left forward Coy. of the Right Front Line Bn. will at once be sent across the footbridge at K.26.A.4.7, and if the bridge over the JARD CANAL at K.26.B.5.6 is still in existence, will cross the Canal and form a Bridgehead on the following line - K.20.A.4.4 - Road Junction, K.20.B.7.7 - Road Junction, K.21.B.0.9 - Road Junction K.21.B.8.3 - Cross Roads, K.22.C.5.1 - Road Junction, K.28.C.1.7 - K.27.D.5.2.

4. This Coy. will, as soon as possible, be followed by the support Coy. of the Front Line Bn. which will be used to strengthen the Bridgehead formed by the leading Coy.

5. In the event of the Bridge at K.26.B.5.6 being destroyed the 412th. Field Coy. R.E. will throw a footbridge across as soon as possible. The construction of this Bridge will be covered by the fire of the leading Coy. of the Front Line Bn. which, in this case, will take up a position on the Western Bank of the Canal on either side of the Bridge to be constructed.
As soon as the Bridge has been completed this Coy. will act as laid down in para. 3.
O.C., Right Front Line Bn. will detail his left supporting Coy. to act as carriers of bridging material for this Section. As soon as the material has been carried forward this Coy. will act as laid down in para. 4.

6. O.C., 412th. Field Coy. R.E., will arrange to have 1 Section standing by ready to proceed forward at short notice to construct the footbridge mentioned in para. 5.
O.C., Section, 412th. Field Coy. R.E., should keep in touch with H.Q., Right Front Line Bn. in order to make the necessary arrangements for carrying out the above orders.

7. As soon as the footbridges have been constructed, and the Bridgehead mentioned in para. 3 has been formed, the support Bn. and 1 Section L.T.M. Battery will cross the ESCAUT and the JARD CANAL, pass through the Bridgehead and advance and make good the line K.29.central - K.16.central. This line will be held with 2 Coys. and the remaining 2 Coys. and H.Q., Bn. will be located in K.22.D.
NOTE. Bn. will not be accompanied by any transport.

8. This Bn. will be followed as soon as possible by the remainder of the Right Front Bn., L.T.M. Battery less 1 Section/

- 2 -

Section and the Left Front Line Bn. in the order mentioned.
After crossing, the above units will concentrate in following areas:-

    Right Front Line Bn.) K.21.D
    L.T.M. Battery   )

    Left Front Line Bn. K.21.B

9. Orders for the concentration of the Left Front Line Bn. and the forward moves mentioned in paras. 7 and 8 will be issued from Bde. H.Q.

10. Two Coys. 52nd. Bn. M.G.C., less transport, under command of O.C., "B" Coy. will follow the support Bn. and will assist in taking up the line mentioned in para. 7 (under orders of O.C., Bn.) with 1 Coy., keeping the remaining Coy. concentrated near Bn. H.Q. in K.22.D.

11. As soon as the above mentioned line has been secured, and pontoon Bridges have been constructed,* mounted troops, consisting of 2 troops, 4th. Hussars and 1 Coy. VIII Corps Cyclist Bn. under orders of O.C., Squadron, 4th. Hussars, will cross the River and Canal, pass through the line K.29.central - K.16.central and secure the following points:-
    (a) MONT OCPIEMONT
    (b) MONT DE PERUWELZ and N.W. exits from BOIS DE LERMITAGE.
    (c) BOUQUET - PERUWELZ Road
* NOTE:- Pontoon Bridges will be constructed under orders of the C.R.E. at the following points:-
  (1) near COUPURE, K.27.D.5.1, to be known as Bridges A and B.
  (2) near PONT DE LA VERNETTE, to be known as Bridges X and Y.

12. These mounted troops will be followed by "A" Battery, 63rd. Bde. R.F.A., who will support the mounted troops but will act independently.

13. On receipt of orders from Bde. H.Q. O.C., support Bn. will move forward with the 2 Coys. concentrated in K.22.D to support the mounted troops mentioned in para. 11 and to take over objectives from them as gained.

14. On receipt of orders from O.C., 52nd. Bn. M.G.C., the 2 Coys. M.G. Bn. mentioned in para. 10 will also move forward in support of the mounted troops.

15. The Northern and Southern Boundaries of the advance will be notified later.

16. First Line Transport will move across the Canal as soon as possible after the Pontoon Bridges have been constructed, and will be sent up to join units in their concentration areas as soon as is practicable.

18. Movements of Bde. H.Q. will be notified later.

                                         Captain,
5th. November 1918.   Brigade Major, 156th. Inf. Bde.

Copies to:- 157th. Inf. Bde   B.T.O.
          155th. Inf. Bde.   O.C., Bde. Sigs.
          174th. Inf. Bde.   1/1st. Low. Fld. Amb.
          52nd. Bn. M.G.C. War Diary (2)
          B.M.   File
          S.C.

```
4th. Royal Scots          412th. Field Coy. R.E    BM 260
7th. Royal Scots          "B" Co. 52nd. Bn. M.G.C.
7th. Sco. Rifles
156th. L.T.M. Battery
```
==

With reference to para. 18 of BM·259 of to-day.

Bde. H.Q. will remain in present position (J.27.D.2.3) until the line K.29.central - K.16.central has been taken up, when it will move to a position about K.21.central (exact location will be notified to all concerned).

An officer from Bde. Staff will be at the Bridge at K.26.A.4.7 during the crossing and until Bde. H.Q. moves. All messages for Bde. H.Q. should be sent to him for transmission.

5th. November 1918.

Captain,
Brigade Major. 156th. Inf. Bde.

```
Copies to:-   157th. Inf. Bde.     B.T.O.
              155th. Inf. Bde.     O.C., Sigs.
              174th. Inf. Bde.     1/1st. L.F.Amb.
              52nd. M.G. Bn.       War Diary (2)
              B.M.                 File
              S.C.
```

O.C.,
4th. Royal Scots
7th. Royal Scots
7th. Sco. Rifles
156th. L.T.M. Battery
"J" Coy. 52nd. Bn. M.G.C. (Group Commander)

SECRET.

BM 263

Continuation of BM 259 of to-day.

1. Pending the issue of further orders the Northern and Southern Boundaries referred to in para. 15 will be a continuation of the present Northern and Southern Bde. Boundaries., viz:-

   Northern Boundary:- K.19.B.8.9 thence along Southern Bank of VERGNE River to Railway at L.7.C.6.8.

   Southern Boundary:- K.33.D.6.2 - K.28.D.2.2 - Railway at L.25.A.8.9 - Road at L.21.D.5.6

2. O.C.,,7th. Royal Scots will gain touch with 157th. Inf. Bde. on our right at the following points:-
   (1) K.29.central
   (2) The CONDE - PERUWELZ Railway at L.25.A.8.9.
   (3) The CONDE - BONSECOURS Road at L.21.D.5.6 in the event of an advance being made <u>through</u> the BOIS DE L'ERMITAGE.

   Definite parties will be told off for the "shaking hand" places, and reports will be sent as soon as touch has been gained.

3. As it appears unlikely that the Bde. on our left will be up in line with us for a considerable period, no actual "shaking hand" places are being laid down, but in the event of their coming into line with us touch will at once be gained by the leading troops and reports rendered to that effect.

5th. November 1918
Captain,
Brigade Major, 156th. Inf. Bde.

Copies to:-
157th. Inf. Bde.
155th. Inf. Bde.
174th. Inf. Bde.
52nd. Bn. M.G.C.
B.M.
S.C.

B.T.O.
O.C., Bde. Sigs.
412th. Field Co. R.E.
War Diary (2)
F110

SECRET.

4th. Royal Scots
7th. Royal Scots
7th. Sco. Rifles
156th. L.T.M. Battery
"B" Coy. 52nd. Bn. M.G.C. (Group Commander)

B.M. 264.

Reference B.M. 259.

1. Reference para. 7.
The line K.29.central – K.16.central will be continued on the right by the 157th. Inf. Bde. along the VIEUX-CONDE Road to Q.6.A.

2. The Reference para. 10.
(a) Two Coys. 52nd. Bn. M.G.C., have been placed definitely under orders of G.O.C., 156th. Inf. Bde.
(b) Two Sections of "C" Coy. will cross the Canal without transport and will assist in taking up the line K.16.central – K.29.central.
(c) "B" Coy. and "C" Coy., less 2 Sections, with transport, will cross the Canal by the Pontoon Bridges after the leading Brigade R.F.A., and will concentrate near Bn. H.Q. in K.22.D.

3. Reference para. 11.
(a) VIII Corps Cyclist Bn., less 1 Coy., are covering the whole of the Divisional front, and will pass over the Canal and River by means of foot bridges as soon as the Right Front Line Bn. has established the Bridgehead mentioned in para. 4.
(b) O.C., Cyclist Bn. will receive his reports through O.C., Support Bn. and has been instructed to keep in close liaison with him.
(c) Two troops, 4th. Hussars, will cross the Canal and River as soon as the Pontoon Bridges have been constructed, and will push on in support of the cyclists mentioned above.
(d) The mounted troops as a whole will make good the following lines on the Divisional front:-

(i) VIEUX CONDE – PERUWELZ Railway, (R.1., L.31., L.25., L.19., L.15.)
(ii) CONDE – MONT DE PERUWELZ – PERUWELZ Road (L.32., L.26., L.20., L.14., L.8.)
(iii) CONDE – CHATEAU DE L'ERMITAGE – BOUQUET Road, (L.33., L.27., L.21., L.13., L.S.B. and D.)
(iv) The line LORETTE – BONSECOURS – PERUWELZ.

4. Paras. 13 and 14 are cancelled and the following substituted:-

On receipt of orders from Bde. H.Q., O.C. Support Bn. will move forward with the 2 Coys. concentrated in K.22.D, and H.Q. and 2 Sections "C" Coy., 52nd. Bn. M.G.C., in order to support the mounted troops mentioned in para. 11, and to take over objectives from them as gained.

5. With the above exceptions B.M. 259, 260 and 263 hold good.

Captain,
Brigade Major, 156th. Inf. Bde.

5th. November 1918.

Copies to:- 157th. Inf. Bde.   B.M.
           155th. Inf. Bde.   S.C.
           174th. Inf. Bde.   B.T.O.
           52nd. Bn. M.G.C.   O.C., Bde. Sigs.
           412th. Field Coy. R.E. Diary (2)
           1/1st. Low. Fld. Amb. File.

"C" Form.
MESSAGES AND SIGNALS.

Army Form C. 2123.
(In books of 100.)

Prefix: B Code: Words: 2120
Charges to Collect:
Service Instructions: Banks Alive

Received. From: WE By: Pol 104
Sent, or sent out. At: app m.
Office Stamp.

Handed in at: .... Office .... m. Received 21.35 m.

TO: 91 SY

Sender's Number: HT 187
Day of Month: 6
In reply to Number:
AAA

Ref	order	57 aaa	Inf
first	line	Transport	will
not	cross	Canal	until
after	artillery	and	Second
Field	Ambulance	with	following
exception	aaa	12 M B	limbers
will	follow	squadron	4th
Hussars	otherwise	M B	lighting
limbers	accompany	their	Batons
aaa	L B	and	SAA limbers
of	leading	Battalion	of
Bde	follow	leading	Bty
58 Bde			

FROM
TIME & PLACE: H Wie

"C" Form.
MESSAGES AND SIGNALS.

Army Form C. 2123.
(In books of 100.)

No. of Message

Prefix: B
Code:
Words:
2129
Charges to Collect
Service Instructions: Priority HWY

Received. From: WE By: B/10H

Sent, or sent out. At: m. To: By:

Received 2125 m.

TO: G4SV

Sender's Number.	Day of Month.	In reply to Number.	AAA
F 31	6		

Btys will cross SCARPE in following order on receipt HUNT aaa 20th 28th D/69 aaa 52 Y A/56 C/56 B/56 aaa 56 Bde Btys will remain position on readiness vicinity J 35 D until Bridges over canal ready aaa all teams and first line wagons will be at Bty Position by 0600 tomorrow aaa 19th Bty should send 1 officer to reconnoitre Q 6.D when Bridge reported still intact aaa 52 Y & D/69 should use our C.P. on hand in Concentration drawing H.F. tonight

FROM / TIME & PLACE: Hives

"C" FORM.
MESSAGES AND SIGNALS.

Prefix **PM** Code **2115** Words **65**
Received from **DA** By **Scott**
Service Instructions **HWE**

Sent, or sent out. At ___ m. To ___ By ___

Office Stamp. **Su 7/11/18**

Handed in at ___ Office ___ m. Received **9.22** m.

TO **Gion**

Sender's Number	Day of Month	In reply to Number	AAA
HT 183	7th		

Ref 52 DA order 51 aaa to help assembly and road control it is notified aaa Bridges will not be ready before four hours afterward HUNT aaa Work will not be carried out on bridges during darkness

FROM **52 DA**
PLACE & TIME

"C" FORM.
MESSAGES AND SIGNALS.

Army Form C. 2121
(In books of 100.)
No. of Message ....

Prefix SB	Code 0853	Words 11	Sent, or sent out.	Office Stamp.
Received from WE	By AJA		At m.	SU
Service Instructions			To	8/11/18
Bty HIWE			By	

Handed in at   Office   m. Received 9A m.

TO YISU HIKO

*Sender's Number	Day of Month.	In reply to Number	AAA
HT180	8th		

RJ DAO 51 HUNT aaa

acknowledge

FROM
PLACE & TIME   HIWE   0850

B.M. 1/13 Appendix IV

155th Inf. Bde. will march tomorrow 11th inst. via HEACHIES D.13.c.0.0, ERBAUT, D.15.d.1.3, D.22.b.central.

Advance Guard, 1/4th R.S.F. (probably one Battery R.F.A., one Coy. M.G. Bn.) under Lieut. C. GIBB.

Main Guard to be about C.18.c.4.0 at 0700.

Main Body, Starting Point I.2.c.5.9.

    Bde. H.Q.   0700
    5th R.S.F.   0701
    4th K.O.S.B.   0707
    Followed by first line transport (less L.G. limbers) in same order of march as units.
    Bearer Section.   0713
    Train Transport   0714.

No halt will be made for breakfasts en route.

Detailed orders will be issued at 0500 to units of this Bde.

Bde. H.Q. will arrange re Battery and M.G. Coy. for Advance Guard.

L.T.M. Sections will join battalions at Starting Points.

Reports to VACRASSE, C.30.c.4.5 after 0700.

ACKNOWLEDGE

[signature] Major,
Bde. Major, 155th Inf. Brigade.

10/11/18.

Copies to -
    4th R.S.F.
    5th R.S.F.
    4th K.O.S.B.
    155 L.T.M. Bty.
    Staff Capt.
    52nd Div.
    156 Inf. Bde.
    157 Inf. Bde.
    C.R.A. 52nd Div. ✓
    218th Coy. A.S.C.
    52nd Bn. M.G.C.
    175 Inf. Bde.
    56 Bde. R.F.A.
    2nd L.F.A.
    File.
    Diary (2).

BELGIUM AND PART OF FRANCE

SHEET 44.

EDITION 3. Provisional until Publication of Edit. 4.

ALL HEIGHTS IN METRES.
CONTOUR INTERVAL 5 METRES.

Scale 1:40,000

Map IV

BELGIUM AND PART OF FRANCE

1:40,000

ALL HEIGHTS IN METRES
CONTOUR INTERVAL 5 METRES

BELGIUM AND PART OF FRANCE SHEET 45.
EDITION 3

Malt

15

shrimp

CONFIDENTIAL

WAR DIARY

of

56TH BRIGADE, R.F.A.

FROM 1st December 1918   TO 31st December 1918

(VOLUME IV. PART XII.)

[signature]
a/ Lieut., Colonel, RFA.
Commanding 56th Brigade, RFA.

WAR DIARY or INTELLIGENCE SUMMARY

56th (1st) Bde RFA Army Form C. 2118.
Vol IV Part XII

Place	Date	Hour	Summary of Events and Information	Remarks and references to Appendices
ERBAUT	1-12-18		Nil	JZ1
	2-12-18		Capt E.S. Walter RFA from Adjutant to Command of A/56. Lt. J. Battery RFA to 2nd Adjutant	JZ1
	3-12		Nil	JZ1
	4-12			
	5-12		1 Cpl 24 Gunners 14 Drivers 4 Bdrs received as reinforcements	JZ1
	6-12		Nil	
	11-12			
	12-12		Bde moved as follows	JZ1
			HQ CASTEAU	Ref: Sheet 45 40000
			A " K&6 80.10
			B St DENIS K11a 60.80
			C CASTEAU L13d 70.00
			527 " E30d 20.30
			E30d 10.10
CASTEAU	13-12		Nil	
	15-12			JZ1
	16-12		1 Sgt 1 S.S. 3 Gunners as reinforcements	JZ1
	17-12		Nil	
	19-12			JZ1
	20-12-18		Reinforcements 1 Sgt 4 1 Cpl received	JZ1

Confidential

WAR DIARY
or
INTELLIGENCE SUMMARY.
(Erase heading not required.)

56th Bde RFA

Army Form C. 2118.

Vol IV Part 12

Place	Date	Hour	Summary of Events and Information	Remarks and references to Appendices
CASTEAU	21-12-18		Lt F. P. Doy posted to 56 Bde RFA. A Battery will effect from 20-12-18	JLJ
	21-12-18		Inspection by G.O.C. 52nd Div	JLJ
	22-12-18 to 26-12-18		NIL	JLJ
	27-12-18		Major A. Black D.S.O. posted to command of 527 Battery R.F.A. 6 Cpl. L 5 Bdrs & 53 Gunners attached from Div Trench Mortars. Major A Tenger assumes the rank of Captain 527 Battery R.F.A. & will perform the duties of Bde Educator	JLJ JLJ
	28-12-18		Lt leaves R.E. Consult Bde Educator Officers 1 O.R. reinforcement received	JLJ JL/
	29-12-18		NIL	JL/
	30-12-18		NIL	
	31-12-18		Infantry parties attached to A & C Batteries returns to 155 Inf Bde. 22 Gunners left for Demob'n Centre No 7 Watford Details	JLJ

Th. Hycry
Lt Col
Comdg 56th Bde R.F.A.

CONFIDENTIAL.

War Diary

of

56th BRIGADE RFA.

from 1st January, 1919   to 31st January, 1919.

(Volume V) Part 1.

Confidential

56th Bde RFA Army Form C. 2118.

Vol 5 Part I

WAR DIARY
or
INTELLIGENCE SUMMARY.
(Erase heading not required.)

Instructions regarding War Diaries and Intelligence Summaries are contained in F. S. Regs., Part II. and the Staff Manual respectively. Title pages will be prepared in manuscript.

Place	Date	Hour	Summary of Events and Information	Remarks and references to Appendices
CASTEAU	Jan 1919 1st		"A" Return	NIL
	2nd		4 O.R's left for demobilization	
	5th		6 O.R's " "	
	9th		5 O.R's " "	
	10th		8 O.R's " "	
	11th		18 O.R's " "	
	12th		2nd Lieut J. L. Marr A/56 Bde R.F.A. and 6 O.R's left for demobilization	
	13th		7 O.R's left for demobilization	
	14th		2nd Lieut G. Lynestoven C/56 Bde R.F.A. struck off the strength on being posted to 261st Bde R.F.A.	
			9 O.R's left for demobilization	
	19th		13 O.R's left for demobilization ←	
	20th		Lieut J. Cocuir H.Q. 57 Bde R.F.A. and 10 O.R's left for demobilization	
	21st		2nd Lieut A/56 Bde RFA and 10 O.R's left for demobilization	
	22nd		2nd Lieut A. Fogg struck off strength to Bde. 20 Horses U.K. whatever	
	28th		18 O.R's left for demobilization	
	31st		15 O.R's left for demobilization	

Copyright

5⟨ Bde RFA Army Form C. 2118.
Vol 5 Part I

WAR DIARY
or
INTELLIGENCE SUMMARY.
(Erase heading not required.)

Place	Date	Hour	Summary of Events and Information	Remarks and references to Appendices
CASTEAU	Jan 27		Major R.H. Howse O/57 Bde R.F.A. and 18 O.R.s left for demobilisation	W/S
	28		16 O.R.s left for demobilisation	W/S
	29		13 O.R.s left for demobilisation	

Mhm Mayor
Comdg 5⟨ Bde RFA

CONFIDENTIAL

War Diary

of

56th. Brigade, R. F. A.

From 1st. February, 1919 to 28th. February, 1919.

Volume 5
Part II

[signature]
a/Lieut.Colonel, RFA
Commanding 56th.Brigade,RFA

Army Form C. 2118.

56th Bde RFA   Vol 5 Part II

WAR DIARY
or
INTELLIGENCE SUMMARY.
(Erase heading not required.)

Instructions regarding War Diaries and Intelligence Summaries are contained in F. S. Regs., Part II and the Staff Manual respectively. Title pages will be prepared in manuscript.

Place	Date	Hour	Summary of Events and Information	Remarks and references to Appendices
CASTEAU	1-2-19		18 other Ranks left for demobilization	
	2-2-19		Nil	
	3-2-19		Ranks left for demobilization	
			14 other Ranks left for demobilization. Lieut Beynon & Butler left for demobilization	
	4-2-19		Nil	
	5-2-19		9 other Ranks left for demobilization	
	6,7,8-2-19			
	9-2-19		Boyce left for demobilization	
	10-2-19		Paterson left for U.K. prior to posting to Palestine	
	11-2-19			
	12-2-19		Nil	
	13-2-19			
	19-2-19		Capt Elliott left for U.K. prior to posting for Palestine	
	20-2-19		6 "Y" animals sent away	
	21-2-19			
	22-2-19		60 "Z" animals sent away	
	23-2-19		3 "Y" animals sent away	
	24-2-19		Nil	
	25,26-2-19		Major A. Black D.S.O. posted 9th Bde RFA	
	27-2-19		Capt R.A. Aiken M.C. posted 527 Bty R.F.A.	
	28-2-19		Nil	

Th Ingram Lieut Col
Commdg 56 Bde RFA

CONFIDENTIAL

War   Diary

    of

56th B R I G A D E, RFA.,

from..1st.March,.1919.   to...31st.March,.1919..

            Volume V

EXTRACT FROM. 52nd D.A. NO. S.C.309.

STATEMENT OF OFFICERS FOR CADRE ETC.,

UNIT	REQUIRED FOR CADRE.	REMARKS.
H.Q.	LT.COL. J.M.Ingram.	
	a/Capt. E. Battersby	Adjutant
A/56	a/MAJOR. E.S. Waller, M.C.	
	2/Lieut. H. Bibby.	
B/56	a/Major. D. Bird, M.C., D.C.M.,	
	2/Lieut. R.D.P.Foxley.	
C/56	Captain. E.C.H.Jensen.	
	Lieut. E.H. Hamlyn	Volunteer for 1 year.
527	a/Capt. W. Wood.	
	Lieut. E.P. Doy.	

56th Brigade R.F.A.

Army Form C. 2118.

WAR DIARY
or
INTELLIGENCE SUMMARY

Vol V   Part III

(Erase heading not required.)

Instructions regarding War Diaries and Intelligence Summaries are contained in F.S. Regs., Part II. and the Staff Manual respectively. Title pages will be prepared in manuscript.

Place	Date	Hour	Summary of Events and Information	Remarks and references to Appendices
CASTEAU	1.3.19		Nil	JLI
	2.3.19		Lt Webb joined from 9th Bde RFA & posted to B Battery	JLI
	3-3-19		25 Z animals to Base	JLI
	4-3-19		Nil	JLI
	5.3.19		Lt-Gunner R.F.A. to England & struck off strength accordingly	JLI
	6.3.19		100 Z animals to Base	JLI
	8.3.19		30 OR's demobilized T. R.F.A. from 9th Bde R.F.A. & posted to command of 527 Battery RFA	JLI
	9.3.19		Capt. T. Wood A/56 Bde R.F.A. posted to 9th Bde RFA. Lt Bibby joined A/56 from C/107 RFA	JLI
	10.3.19		Lt Brown A/56 Bde R.F.A. posted to Base. 38 Z animals to sale SOIGNIES	JLI
	11.3.19		4 Z mules to Base	JLI
	12.3.19		22 Z animals from 9th Bde on 10th and posted to Rhine on the 13th	JLI
	13.3.19		Lt Winship joined from 9th Bde RFA. 6Z animals to SOIGNIES	JLI
			69 OR's to Rhine	JLI
	14.3.19		Nil	JLI
	15.3.19		3 OR's to Rhine to England & struck off Strength	JLI
	16.3.19		Capt Anchor R.F.A.	JLI
	17.3.19		Nil 7 OR's demobilized. Bde concentrated in SOIGNIES	JLI
	18.3.19		7 Gunners to Rhine	JLI
	19.3.19		Nil	JLI
	20.3.19		68 X mules to COLOGNE The attached S.C. 309 gives officers for Cadre	H JLI
	21.3.19		Nil	JLI
	22.3.19		30 OR's & 1 Farr. Sgt. 68 X horses to 9th Bde	JLI
	23.3.19		Nil	JLI
	24.3.19		Nil	JLI
	25.3.19		1 BQMS to 147 Bde R.F.A.	JLI
	26.3.19		1 Sgt to D.A.C. Hunt RFA to U.K. for demobilization	JLI
	27.3.19		Capt Barnes & Capt Hunt RFA to U.K. for demobilization	JLI
	28.3.19		Nil	JLI
	29-3-19		Nil	JLI
	30-3-19		27 OR's to 9th Bde RFA	JLI
	31-3-19		5 OR's to D.A.C.	JLI

Th Longuet
Lt Col
56th Bde RFA